Images of Kin

Books by Michael S. Harper

Images of Kin
Nightmare Begins Responsibility
Debridement
Song: I Want a Witness
Photographs: Negatives: History as Apple Tree
History Is Your Own Heartbeat
Dear John, Dear Coltrane
Heartblow: Black Veils *(editor)*

Images of Kin

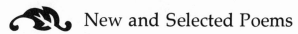 New and Selected Poems

Michael S. Harper

University of Illinois Press

Urbana Chicago London

Library of Congress Cataloging in Publication Data

Harper, Michael S
   Images of kin: new and selected poems.

   I. Title.
   PS3558.A6248I5   811'.5'4   77-24932
   ISBN 0-252-00606-2
   ISBN 0-252-00607-0 pbk.

Thanks are due to the editors of the periodicals in which the following poems first appeared: "Crossing Lake Michigan," "Bristol: Bicentenary Remembrances of Trade," "Smoke," "The Battle of Saratoga (Springs) Revisited," "Dining from a Treed Condition," "The Founding Fathers in Philadelphia," "Psychophotos of Hampton," 1977, *Massachusetts Review*; "Cannon Arrested," 1976, *New Letters*; "Healing Song" (originally titled "Healing Song for Robert Hayden"), 1976, *Yardbird Reader*; "Made Connections," 1977, *American Poetry Review*; "Tongue-Tied in Black and White" (originally titled "Remembering John Berryman") and "Eve (Rachel)," 1975, *Field*.

Some of the poems in this book were drawn from *Nightmare Begins Responsibility* (1975) and *History Is Your Own Heartbeat* (1971), which were published by the University of Illinois Press.

The poems from *Debridement* were published in 1973 by Doubleday and Co., Inc.

The poems from *Dear John, Dear Coltrane* (© 1970 by University of Pittsburgh Press) and *Song: I Want a Witness* (© 1972 by Michael S. Harper) are reprinted by permission of the University of Pittsburgh Press.

A friend told me
he'd risen above jazz.
I leave him there.

for my family, extended and whole,
a love supreme

and in memory of my brother,
Jonathan Paul Harper, 1941–1977

Contents

VII   from *Dear John, Dear Coltrane*

Part I

Healing Songs

the tongue is the customer of the ear

Crossing Lake Michigan

The amp light on the station
wagon has just gone out;
we climb up the hatch-stairs
to the deck, the clouds mildewed
as storms move east, bucketing
the interstate with torrential rain.
The ferry bucks my daughter's soft
forehead into my neck, dreaming,
perhaps of strawberry patches
she investigates for bright
spots ripening as she skips
the white; late one August evening
she appeared lost for hours
as storm clouds rocked
in rowboats moving in swirls
of leaves under lakeside elms;
when she was discovered, her rear-
end skyward, bent, we foraged for pure
red signals of strawberry.

I brush her hair back from her face
so similar to my sister's at the same age,
smile, though I overhear two Michigan
tourists, returning home, talk of menace
of cities, how King asked for glory
of newsprint and ate the balcony railing
in conspiracy of his lost appetite;

I think of amp lights that will ignite
our three darkened hours to Ann Arbor,
a call made to an all-night self-service
garage where you can buy parts.

She wakes with songs learned from her teacher,
her mother trailing a lawnmower of seeds
on the furrowed lawn, catching the tune
of a great thrush lock-stepped in imitation.
His one song of politics, the power of the ferry
climbing swells to a future of hungry birds
lost in Michigan, where a strike wavers near a highway
I will go by: she will ask for the strawberry's whiteness,
and why men will not eat at her table of red,
and what song to sing to vacationers returning to
   Michigan.

Conferences with the Unknown

'. . . in another way the shocking and absurd disjunction of the Western towns and whatever natural environment has been permitted to survive around them: Colorado Springs, for example, with its pretentious "downtown," its hopeless grids of suburban bungalows—mocked and dwarfed by the solemnity of Pike's Peak.'

—Frederick W. Turner III, "Strangers in America,"
The Nation, 2 Oct. 76

After working through, all day,
the meaning of 'minority'
we go through the circles of snow,
fluxed faces of students,
the oval staked college walk;
one looks up to see the peaks snowed over
with recent flurries, the feathered firs
luring dark eyes to the trail of tears;
the lined penciled drawings of postcard
highlights the portages in Dunbar stamps.

We portage this swimming pool
in pelted reflections, our silhouettes
the slick elegance of gutters
gurgling in bloodless chlorine
stinging our eyes as the lime
shutters down on the bodies
of children beaten in the arms
of the mothers at Sand Creek,
the battleground we will not visit
while we wait, rushing, for our plane.

Trails leading to Idaho, Wyoming
parks cut by forest reservations,
furrowed in death-songs, each bier
raked over and over to light
banked snows of the snowplow;

in a van seating fifteen
we carom, gorge to gorge,
in the transfixed charts
leading to Air Force Academy,
where the chapel opens in prayer
to pilots still lost over Cambodia.
Signs bumpered in crayon
ask their return,
sighted in these highlands
by hungry widows, their starched vigilance
forgotten in the eyes of their children
encircling secret files in the Pentagon.

On an air force runway in California
the faces of consulate children peer
into the irised dittos of the cameras:

Geronimo's at St. Louis
World's Fair, his pocked broken jaw
addles silently to drunken laughter,
high on exhaust from the new Ford
mud-stuck on the Mississippi;
on horseback, and seventy-five,
he rides through the slave quarters
campsoaked in thunderclaps of rain,
his sons lost in the campaigns of Mexico
bandage the broken neck of the pinto
in the foothills of the Platte;

what runways he sees in the eyes
of fairground keepers, the tollgate
portages of Pleiku and Mojave
vaccinate in broken words in Colorado.

Cannon Arrested

Somethin' Else and
Kind of Blue
bleed back to back
as the Cannon arrests,
his V-shaped heart
flowing in glycerine
compounds of fixed signs
stabilized in his going:
who helps him as he softshoes
starstreamed joculars across
each throated arch of song,
stylings of separation?

His fat silent reed
beds down in Gary,
shanked by Stevie Wonderful's
moment of silence,
these mosquito whinings
near the liter can of gas
I pour into Buick 59.

In some unmarked Floridian grave
another ancestor shakes
to your damnation,
her son perhaps pulling a giant
sailboat behind his Cadillac
to sporty Idlewild, Michigan,
sanctified in attitudes
of 'Dis Here' on this side of the road,
'Dat Dere' *going over* on that side,
and the boat docks before me
in distant transformed banks
of you transporting this evil
woman's song pianola-ed
on Interstate 80, cardiac bypass

road-turn you didn't make,
your fins sailing over boundaries,
lined fingertips in a reefered house,
a divided storehouse near a black
resort town, this sweet alto-man
wickered in vestibule, drifting away.

Tongue-Tied in Black and White

—'I had a most marvelous piece of luck. I died.'

In Los Angeles
while the mountains cleared of smog
your songs dreamed
Jefferson and Madison
walking hand in hand
as my grandfather walked to Canada.
What eyes met the black student
next to me, her hands fanning
your breezy neck from this veranda,
but Henry's/Mr. Bones.

Home from Mexico and you in LIFE,
I walk dead center into the image
of LBJ cloistered by the draping
flags of Texas and the confederacy,
and as my aunt of Oklahoma told me
I understand your father's impulse
to force you into Crane's nightmare.

After the Roethke reading in Seattle
you stroked the stout legs of an ex-
student's wife while he sketched
you in adoration and as you cautioned
your audience, '45 minutes and no longer,'
how Harvard paid in prestige not money,
how a man at Harvard read for four hours,
that he ought to be set down in the Roman
courtyard and have rocks set upon him
until death—your audience laughed.

You admired my second living son
as you loved the honeyed dugs of his mother,

your spotless tan suit weaving in the arch
where goalposts supported you in foyer
for you would not fall.

At your last public reading,
let out for fear of incident without a drink,
your foot bandaged from fire you'd
stamped out in a wastebasket of songs,
your solitary voice speckled in Donne,
in Vermont where the stories of Bread
Loaf, Brown, another broken leg abandoned
in monotones of your friends studying you;

Now I must take up our quarrel:
never dangerous with women
though touched by their nectared hair,
you wrote in that needful black idiom
offending me, for only your inner voices
spoke such tongues, your father's soft prayers
in an all black town in Oklahoma; your ear lied.
That slave in you was white blood forced to derision,
those seventeenth-century songs saved you from
   review.

Naked, in a bottle of Wild Turkey,
the bridge you dived over was your source:
St. Paul to St. Louis to New Orleans,
the *asiento*, Toussaint, border ruffians,
signature of Lincoln, porters bringing
messages to white widows of Europe,
a classics major, and black, taking your classes,
the roughpage of your bird legs and beard
sanitizing your hospital room,
the last image of your bandaged foot
stamping at flames on the newborn bridge.

This is less than the whole truth
but it is the blacker story
and what you asked to be told:
'lay off the sauce when you write'
you said to me, winking at the brownskinned
actress accompanying me to the lectern;
and how far is Texas from Canada
and our shared relatives in blacktown
on the outskirts of your tongue, tied still.

Eve (Rachel)

'What has gone into that quality of voice, that distancing, that precise knowledge of who she is, where she has come from, what costs have been to herself, but also to others, the ones who did not survive.'

'the rib is but the unseen potential aspect of self, free of fleshly desire, waiting to be discovered, to be named beyond definition, a conjugation of names in deeds.'

I have been waiting to speak to you
for many years; one evening
I sat down to tell the story
of your mother's song of *Fante*,
"The Dance of the Elephants"
on the lips of her parents
escaping in disguise.
From this ribbed podium I have waited
for you to join my own daughter,
Rachel, in the arena of surrender,
where women bathe the wounds
in our dark human struggle to be human:
this must be earned in deeds.

There are blessings to remember:
your magical birth on the third
anniversary of your parents' wedding.
I was there among the family faces
strung on violin and cello,
your Irish grandmother's song of the bogs,
your hidden grandfather's raging at your loveliness,
at his own daughters swimming amidst swans.

I talk of you to your parents over these distancings,
our voices rising over gray Portland skies,
the lush green of your eyes
shuttered in springtime;

you can not be otherwise than your grandmothers'
healing songs sprouting through you,
a tree in essential bloom in standing water.

To be here in America?
Ask this of the word many times:
in your parents' books underlined in green,
in dark blotches of your life-giving womb,
in these riddles beckoning—
'old folk songs chanted underneath the stars,'
in the cadence of black speech:
'just like a tree; backwater, muddy water,'
in gentle eyes of these writers of kinship,
in the circle of light which is Little Crow,
skinned and diced folksaying his splintered story,
comforts in small utterances, remember,
Eve means rescue from bodily desire.

Our last welcome
is the love of liars
in tall tales to larger truths;
succor these voices in your blood
listening for doubletalk, stoicism, irony
where your heart-center funnels its loam,
where you will plant your own crafted shoes
in these bodies of soiled, broken, mending hands.

Healing Song

He stoops down eating sunflowers
snowballed at his prayer-rugged
table, 'message/solution/masses'
his ghetto-blues-plantation,
driven into inner/outer realities
as buffers drawn from his eyes.

Penned in that magnificent voice
where *victorola* mutters 'Koppin' songs,
his sedge burning night-trains,
this serape-man found wanting
only in that 'God Don't Like Ugly'
phrase; he draws his own lightning,
believing differently,
an angel surrendering angles of desire:
his masked heart-centered soul reveals.

Rused in dance steps of jubilo,
atavisms of worship shutting out sound,
his full essential flowering
balances in the 4 a.m. traduction,
his Emancipation Tree.

Hidden in ancient tetters
of autobiography,
he tropes of 1863 *moverings*,
his Osceolas already sacrificed
as Lincoln's mass production lines
funnel bodies to the Crater;
his Easter families agonize
at blue doors of transformation.

Self-accused in venial sins, his gorgeous
offerings lift blind pigs to Bessie's
witchdoctoring, her blue-black tongue
singing down Jesus,
'watch your goin' be like comin' back,'
he witnesses flesh pull down in anger,
killing calves of hunger to no higher law.

Ragboned Bob Hayden, shingled in slime,
reaches for his cereus ladder of midnight flight,
his seismographic heartbeats
sphinctered in rhiney polygraphs of light;
Dee-troit born and half-blind
in diction of arena and paradise,
his ambient nightmare-dreams streak his tongue;
mementos of his mother, of Erma, he image-makes
peopling the human family of God's mirror,
mingling realities, this creature of transcendence
a love-filled shadow, congealed and clarified.

The Wisdom of Signs

A week's gone since the memorial,
taps played, the American
flag presented to your stablemate
knobby-nosed-Ruth-twiddling-liverspotted-fingers;
details of your passing,
birthdate, farm, resort cowering
in tales from six children at death hour:

a well-oiled, primed motor goes dead;
a mink ascends from weeds to dock
where a fishing pole lingers;
thud of grandson's softball
bat ripping seams, a sodden ball.

I look to the single heron
squawking in eastward flight
at first utterance of your name
calling sun from darkness,
light, shade, raindrops
shake from sky over family;
your maple shading
the pastor's table begins to fade:
one's need to blossom passes
to single apple in your solitary
tree; unpicked to fight amidst cedars,
the fruit falls
to swirling coverings of oak leaves.

Though your brother asks for your pictures,
your mother's mementos spartle child images
to the obit column in St. James;
six children hover in this interface
parceling things for departure;
your wife asking for nothing.

In a dream a year from now,
your accounts held
to state and government,
your renegade homestead
contracts in wallet-thin folds
of a dress shirt she will wear;
the anatomy department has sent
your urned ashes in forced march
to Fort Snelling's open furrow;

But I will ponder heart centered
real organ of perception
attacked and flushed in explosion
as you bled over broken teeth,
your nose phalanged into breathlessness,
the meaning of this *conscious* act
bypassed in love of knowledge,
unflagged blossom dying into fruit,
your single apple sweetened
in your mate's hand,
her heart eternalized in your name.

Made Connections

'the wages of dying is love'—Galway Kinnell

Rich with gifts on your return to Edinburgh
your voice quakes in sayable poems chiming
images of your ancestors, the kite in the eye
drawn off into highland village of first
offerings, the misspelt bookmarker for *Alex
Kinell, 1843*, given by his beloved; your gandfather's
snuffbox made from horn into an animal
full of snuff, the gift-bible of the pastor
to your father on his first trip to this city:
all these caretaken by a yawning ninety-year-old
aunt, your relatives rolling in the omphalos
dreams of castles, high manors of war in words.

We sit awhile in first-class bypassing derailment,
the sea suggesting your father's ship, crestfallen
with his leaving homelands for the Boer War;
I open the paper to a photo of a black man bleeding
at the feet of a South African policeman, his boots
caked in riots; one schoolboy locked in a room
littered with corpses, babies and old grannies
moaning on litters, chants his lessons in Afrikaan
begging to get out; the train lumbers on thick with
    uniformed
cadets in fatigues on their way to maneuvers.

Locked in trenches of France and Belgium,
or jumping ship in West Virginia with a friend,
your father makes cabinets as his son makes
testimony in stones, images scribbled on a rocking
train, the image of kite being drawn off into the
    Hebrides,

or the village where a young girl gave the gift of passing
hours, her tongue forcing books to give up light
knowing he would come back to read to an old
woman, of war and travel, the comfort of a sleepy
child, in the moon-arms of her father, made in America.

Bristol: Bicentenary Remembrances of Trade

'Shuttles in the rocking loom of history,
the dark ships move, the dark ships move,
their bright ironical names
like jest of kindness on a murderer's mouth;
. . .
Voyage through death,
                    voyage whose chartings are unlove.'
                            —Robert Hayden, "Middle Passage"

'I wish to be a Member of Parliament
to have my share of doing good or resisting evil.'
                    —Edmund Burke, speech at Bristol, 1780

Though I stand before these words
I don't remember your real aims
of evil or good, my ancestors
don't know either, though I read
at local libraries about your Bristol,
the great fleets skiffing along wave-
tops, cries of kinsmen below,
great schools of sharks forming a crescent
in caravans of corpses buffered in chains.

I buy a handbook for the great events
of this city, post six postcards
to friends, prepare to read of
"Jesus, Estrella, Esperanza, Mercy:
Desire, Adventure, Tartar, Ann:"
the great testimonial to complicity in voices
of excuse for the triangular trade.

I visit a center called "Ink Works,"
where two black Jamaicans paint the day-
nursery, go up to the rec hall for orange
crush, the converted factory of ink

blossoming under grants from agencies
of self-help and annoyance
for the numbers of St. Paul are small.

In the hotel, in a heatwave that goes on
a second week of air-stagnation
and *mooing* trains, the talk is of drought,
crops burning in the midlands, the Avon
buoying the crafts in convergence with sea;
one could tour the 18th-century mansions
or sip some Bordeaux wine in the air-conditioned
bar, or put on a tie for some roastbeef and pie;

on a corner near the exiting uniforms of soldiers
taking shots of "head on the nail,"
the corn riots billow up on screens
of sails on returning ships,
their holds half-empty, the efficient ship-
owners in Liverpool where the moon lifts
and two uniformed Africans carry banners
announcing a ball. The train to Paddington
is quick, hot-shades cover the windows
from a setting sun; newspapers gleam
in smeared headlines of Soweto, my black
baggage hangs on the rack above my head
as I rock to waystation in London
and the transport home to old shores
in Rhode Island.

Smoke

Smoke is my name for you,
gray crystalline hammocks
of smoke in your scowls
wavering over linoleum
of flowers making bread
to kill the starter
yeast in a cold oven,
your thoughts on film,
prints of my daughter
in the playhouse quick
of fire in framed song
memorized as a puzzle,
in the making of bread
in nine unbasted tins.

In a new crafted darkroom,
your hands swimming
in the six-foot sink
fiberglassed over planks
of wood as the coffin
of your father, whose heart
turns in the suturing fingers
of a medical student
learning of thrombosis,
your hands throb the images
with old chemicals that won't
work their magic
of bringing back his face,
his top shelf of broken
teeth caving in,
his thick fingers poised
at his beltbuckle,
your last sigh
like his, slightly bloody

on the top lip,
sink where the heart
leaps in the dusty manure
of horses, his loose boots,
the lunch eaten in chatter
churning no more.

A new batch of dough
rises in tins to such comfort
of the heated oven;
an image bakes in the body
of the six-foot sink,
and when he stands up
in your enlarger
he will ask for butter,
cut you the heel,
look for the jam
as if to light a match
in the name of smoke,
demanding his spot
in your photo album.

Part II

Uplift from a Dark Tower

*"Those who profess to favor Freedom, and yet depre-
cate agitation, are men who want crops without plow-
ing up the ground. . . . Power concedes nothing with-
out a demand."*
—Frederick Douglass

*"Because in a day when the human mind aspired to a
science of human action, a history and psychology of
the mighty effort of the mightiest century, we fell
under the leadership of those who would compromise
with truth in the past in order to make peace in the
present and guide policy in the future."*
—W. E. B. Du Bois

*"The presentation of facts, on a high, dignified plane,
is all the begging that most rich people care for. . . . It
is easily possible that some of my former owners might
be present to hear me speak."*
—Booker T. Washington

The Battle of Saratoga (Springs) Revisited

Just when I think I've got you nailed
to your cross of uplift
I see your name in the private printing
of a history of *Yaddo*,
meaning 'shadow' or 'shimmering,'
its 500-acre testimonial to lakes
over gardens, trees
buried with *lost* children
whose memory donated this tower
studio to my writing of you.

Outside the door might lie *Etienne*,
the cannibal brought by missionaries
from Africa to be trained for service
in the experimental summer of 1881.
He would be St. Patrick to Yaddo's Ireland
handling snakes, woodland spiders,
as simple playthings, his station
outside this room, asleep at threshold,
his carving knife, guarding me safely from exit.
Such loyalty, devotion might lie in
pure strain of his cannibal ancestry:
"my body may be black but my soul is white."

He went back to Africa as a trader.

Dining from a Treed Condition, An Historical Survey

*'in order to be successful in any kind of undertaking, I think the main thing is
for one to grow to the point where he completely forgets himself; that is, to lose
himself in a great cause.'*

At the dinner table where you sat with Peabody,
stirred by the shrewd handicap of scholars and savants,
you opened your certain ginger face
"I was born a slave," rolling jordanized,
accomplished in freedom of all pride,
of all bitterness of a handicapped race
made really safe from Democracy,
the *Trask* check slipped in loamed black
cloth in many dinner wallets of conversation.

I look out the Tower window over the sun-dial
of Etienne's savage memory carved in blue spruce
and the rainbowed cypress hearing Christmas prayers
of Barhyte's slaves, Thom Campbell, his wife, Nancy,
quartered in clear pieces of Bear Swampground
southeast of the Rose Garden, conjuring amused
comic tales of Tom Camel's unselfish episodes
of tree-climbing and masquerade.

Told to saw off a limb on Mr. White's place
he sat on the limb vigorously sawing the obstructing
branch; dazed after a loud crack, on the ground
Tom cried to Mr. White: 'Oh, no Sah! I had the good
fortune to land on mah head';
dressed up in carriage, in woman's clothes,
Camel posed as Burr's Mistress in Stone's
"Reminiscences of Saratoga," as Madame Jumel on one
    of her
visits in 1849, in *criminal* intimacy, at US Hotel,
threatened, bribed, as she followed her counterfeit
double, Tom Camel, fanning himself, curtseying

to crowds on every side to the lakefront with Burr.
(Poor Hamilton never had a chance at masquerade;
Burgoyne, Benedict Arnold cavort on Saratoga field.)

Tales of remembrance, of master and slave,
of mistress, of American patriot in the French style,
take me through statuary, rock and rose gardens,
lakes named for children, concola, white pines
as 'spiritual linguist,' the shadow of Yaddo's
pine and rose on thresholds of cypress, the hanging tree
where Mohawks worshipped
and Camel's chained image swung to ground,
a head injury of couffered masquerade.

The caned walking stick
I borrow from bicycle paths
in metaphor for your whipping to early death,
inviting Madame Jumel perhaps,
your huge clothesbasket full of checks,
the *exposition* address
marketed in cottonballs of fleeced gowns
in a dining hall
where the surprise party
was held on the burned ashes of this rainbow.

The Founding Fathers in Philadelphia

*'some of the questions he asked about the Negro church denominations were:
the number of communicants, the percentage of male and female members, the
seating capacity of the churches, the value of the parsonages, and the total
collection of the African Methodist Episcopal Missionary Department from
1904 to 1908. Again, there was no connection drawn between any of the
material offered in 1909 and the data given in the earlier v's.'*

Meeting in secret, with my great
grandfather AME bishop in Philadelphia,
just before his debarking the ship
from South Africa, I see the choices
for education and literacy of a *downtrodden* people
flushed down the outlet of the ocean
liner, where my earmarked greatgrand
fluxed precious diamonds from the Zulu
chiefs, before stolen by customs.

What tongues did the diamonds speak?
To be educated by black spiritual linguists
from runaway Canada
or the pontiffs of paternity
in the plazas of Saratoga,
I remind myself with a visit to harnessed
racing, no single black jockey present,
for this is even betting handicapped
at fifty dollars and my best thoroughbred
in August, where the Indian spirits
praise a five-hundred-year-old tree
nourished by sacred spring water,
its radioactivity signs ignored,
the freed slave runaways
paddling down the Hudson to Catskill
to the dayline my grandfather ran
before the bridge to Kingston
took his house, his children, to Brooklyn.

Psychophotos of Hampton

   . . .in all fairness to Washington we must recall that Armstrong, in effect,
gave Washington his career.'
                                                        —Robert B. Stepto

Dining at 8 and 6:30
with a lunchpail for noon,
I type out the echoes of artist
in the high studio of the tower,
blackened in the image of Etienne,
his cannibal ancestry sharpened
by the sloped Adirondacks toward Montreal
where French/Indian alliances of beaver pelts
end in burrows of buffalo on open plains,
another mountain range to cross, the salt lick
of lake claiming runaway bigamists,
and the great Sioux herds on the run to Cody,
named for the diseased man who died in Denver,
his widow offered forty grand to be buried near his name.

On a ride down 9W to Esopus, New York,
where Wiltwyck boys from five boroughs
came to the Roosevelt mansion-estate, the volunteers
driving buses with Menonnite alms, to home visits
of abandoned projects, each welfare roll breaking
in fired windows, I take the granite sites
of General Armstrong into view, his great twin
burial rocks, Vermont granite, Sandwich lava
entrancing the mausoleum of the great divide
of history, of railroad lands, of the *Dakotah*,
Sandwich missions, the uplift of schoolmarms
tuning the pens of the Freedmen's Bureau toward
the thin line of traintrack near Emancipation Tree.

At $68/head, the great Dakotah nation went to college,
from Black Hills to mosquitoed swamp near Fort Monroe,
where the fevered zeal of the government

reimbursed each Indian with black suit,
haircut, and a class photograph:

I walk out over swampgrounds, campsites,
drumbeats of the great cemetery
surrounded by sane spirits of the great mansion
at Arlington where Robert E. Lee's doorstep
sprouted with Union graves terraced from his veranda:

For Daniel Fire-Cloud, Sioux, South Dakotah
died September 3 1886, 14 years
Armstrong Firecloud, Sioux, born Hampton
died August 6 1886 infant
Virginia Medicine-Bull, Sioux, South Dakotah
died January 30 1886
Simon Mazakutte, Sioux, South Dakotah
died March 26 1884, 18 years
Benjamin Bear-Bird, Sioux, South Dakotah
died August 4 1885, aged 2 years
Edith Yellow-Hair, Sioux, South Dakotah
died November 26 1885, aged 8 years
Emma Whips, Sioux, South Dakotah
died March 25 1885
Lora Bowed-Head Snow, Sioux, South Dakotah
died March 20 1885, aged 22 years
Mary Pretty-Hair, Sioux, South Dakotah
died January 6 1885, aged 14 years
Eva Good-Road, Sioux, South Dakotah
died January 4 1884, aged 17 years
Belany Sayon-Sululand, South Africa
died December 10 1884, aged 22 years
Edward Buck, Sioux, South Dakotah
died May 30 1884, aged 17 years
Croaking Wing, Mandan, North Dakotah
died April 21 1884, aged 17 years

Francesca Rios, Papago, Arizona
died August 21 1883, aged 15 years
Henry Kendall Acolehut, Yuma, Arizona
died August 13 1883, aged 22 years
Tasute White Back, Gros Ventre, North Dakotah
died January 24 1882, aged 15 years.
I leave out fully anglicized names,
some duplications among the Sioux (meaning dog)
for fear of repeat of the Dakotah.
Buried in graveyards of the great founding
academies, their souls finally saved
from highlands where they were born.
The great Lincoln train
winds into great centennial avenues
where each kneeled slave has the great veil
lifted from his eyes, his enlightened
face literate from heart to mind,
penciled in nightmare,
where the rainbow mansion,
tiered rose garden, Bearground Swamp
vessels the dark interior
of this book I write of the Shadow,
Unjungian and unsurveyed,
in the cleaning of your first bedroom,
over and over the coaldust you brought
under fingernails
as you scratched toward the caning
which would take your exhibition,
your address of the great ship,
its crew calling for water,
clear-watered-buckets-scooping-downward
in five equally broken fingers.

Separate as the limed hand
the five great Indian nations

disappear along the trail
of tears, the common man of Andrew
Jackson looking moonstruck in black regiments
for the Seminoles of Florida,
each Catholic outpost
St. Paul's reservation of Little Crow
waiting for rations,
the St. Louis Fair
where Geronimo breathed the gas
from the Ford caught in the mud
gatewayed in his western eyes,
to New Orleans, where the musicians
stomp all night to Buster's for breakfast,
the buildings boarded up with slave anklets,
the militia protecting the war ships
of Toussaint in Napoleon's gift to Jefferson.

Your simplest image was the crab-barrel,
each black hand pulling the escaping soul
back into the pit where the turpentine
gangs sang, cutting their way through each
wilderness, each Indian amulet dropping
in cross-fires of settlers,
your great dining hall opening:
"I was born a slave,"
countered by Aristotle's
'some men are natural born slaves,'
in the boards of Wall Street,
where Melville wrote the dark glimmerings
scrimshaw tales, attached by the whale,
his bludgeoned knife raised in combat,
his sweat in the oiled battle with self,
where the nation stormed in fish beds
as laughing men and women dove
in triangular trade winds.

The last view is the best,
from the terrace overhang,
with a toothbrush,
seeing rock gardens and roses
pool in cascading fountains:
the Renaissance built on slave trading,
Etienne proud of his lineage,
Booker T's bookings humbling his beginnings,
the abstract masks giving off power,
its conjured being dynamized in my skin,
reminiscing at the founder's table
where the talk was of politics,
rhetoric, and the literature of the great
rainbowed swamp from the vision of the black tower.

Part III

from *Nightmare Begins Responsibility*

the responsibility to nightmare is to wake up

Kin

When news came that your mother'd
smashed her hip, both feet caught
in rungs of the banquet table,
our wedding rebroken on the memory
of the long lake of silence
when the stones of her body
broke as an Irish fence of stones,
I saw your wet dugs drag
with the weight of our daughter
in the quick of her sleep
to another feeding;
then the shoulders dropped
their broken antenna branches
of fear at the knife
running the scars
which had borne into the colon
for the misspent enema,
the clubbed liver unclean
with the stones of the gall bladder,
and the broken arch of hip
lugging you to the lake,
the dough inner tube of lading
swollen with innerpatching.

I pick you up from the floor
of your ringing fears, the floor
where the photographs you have worked
into the cool sky of the gray you love,
and you are back at the compost pile
where the vegetables burn,
or swim in the storm of your childhood,
when your father egged you on with his
open machinery, the exhaust choking your sisters,
and your sisters choked still.

39

Now his voice stops you in accusation,
and the years pile up on themselves
in the eggs of your stretched sons,
one born on his birthday, both dead.
I pull you off into the sanctuary
of conciliation, of quiet tactics,
the uttered question, the referral,
which will quiet the condition you have seen
in your mother's shadow, the crutches
inching in the uncut grass,
and the worn body you will carry
as your own birthmark of his scream.

Landfill

Loads of trash and we light the match;
what can be in a cardboard box
can be in the bed of the pickup
and you jostle the containers onto the side road.
A match for this little road,
and a match for your son riding next to you firing,
and a match for the hole in the land filled with trees.
I will not mention concrete because theirs is the meshed
wire of concrete near the docks, and the concrete
of burned trees cut in cords of change-sawing,
and we will light a match to this too.

Work in anger for the final hour of adjustment
to the surveyors, and to the lawyers speaking of squatting,
and the land burning to no one.
This building of scrap metal, high as the storm that will
break it totally in the tornado dust,
and to the animals that have lived in the wheathay of
    their bedding
will beg for the cutting edge, or the ax,
or the electrified fencing that warms them in summer rain.

My son coughs on the tarred scrubble of cut trees,
and is cursed by the firelight, and beckoned to me to the
    pickup,
and washed of the soot of his sootskinned face,
and the dirt at the corners of my daughter's mouth will
    be trenchmouth;
and the worn moccasin of my woman will tear into the
    bulbed big toe,
and the blood will be black as the compost pile burning,
and the milk from her dugs will be the balm for the
    trenchmouth,
as she wipes her mouth from the smoke of the landfill
    filled with fire,
and these loads of trash will be the ashes for her to take:
and will be taken to the landfill, and filled, and filled.

From a Town in Minnesota

"GUN: *'from the feminine in which both names mean* WAR'"

One side tight in the case,
scope screwed on my head,
brown stock like my owner
unfiring, prepared;
bought from deadly shot
who went berserk in Newport,
I crept into Oakland
in a back seat
of a friend
who later gave up games
with dumdum shell
in his temple
but I was sleeping
on this top shelf
cuddled from explosion.

You want to borrow
me for a hunt
in Kenai,
and uncased
I loosen my handle
sight off center
tightening my strap
on your blade of flesh
I will hold on long
treks through berries
where the moose lie.

I go back to sleep
carried over frontiers
of clothing I lie among,
my master's grandfather
naked on the firing

range, his blue hat
broken at brim;
and know I will
awaken decades from here,
waiting for answers
that never speak to me,
cartridges
of an enemy
part stranger,
greased, armpit anchored,
waiting for the burned flit
of hair trigger
pulled toward the closet,
these skeletons I wear.

Called

Digging the grave
through black dirt,
gravel and rocks
that will hold her down,
we speak of her heat
which has driven her out
over the highway
in her first year.

A fly glides from her mouth
as we take her four legs,
and the great white neck
mudded at the lakeside
bends gracefully into the arc
of her tongue, colorless, now,
and we set her in the bed
of earth and rock
which will hold her as the sun
sets over her shoulders.

You had spoken of her brother,
100 lbs or more,
and her slight frame
from the diet of chain
she had broken;
on her back
as the spade cools her brow
with black dirt, rocks,
sand, white tongue,
what pups does she hold
that are seeds unspayed
in her broken body;
what does her brother say
to the seed gone out over

the prairie, on the hunt
of the unreturned:
and what do we say
to the master of the dog dead,
heat, highway, this bed
on the shoulder
of the road west
where her brother called, calls.

Grandfather

In 1915 my grandfather's
neighbors surrounded his house
near the dayline he ran
on the Hudson
in Catskill, NY
and thought they'd burn
his family out
in a movie they'd just seen
and be rid of his kind:
the death of a lone black
family is *the Birth
of a Nation,*
or so they thought.
His 5'4" waiter gait
quenched the white jacket smile
he'd brought back from watered
polish of my father
on the turning seats,
and he asked his neighbors
up on his thatched porch
for the first blossom of fire
that would burn him down.

They went away, his nation,
spittooning their torched necks
in the shadows of the riverboat
they'd seen, posse decomposing;
and I see him on Sutter
with white bag from your
restaurant, challenged by his first
grandson to a foot-race
he will win in white clothes.

I see him as he buys galoshes
for his railed yard near Mineo's
metal shop, where roses jump
as the el circles his house
toward Brooklyn, where his rain fell;
and I see cigar smoke in his eyes,
chocolate Madison Square Garden chews
he breaks on his set teeth,
stitched up after cancer,
the great white nation immovable
as his weight wilts
and he is on a porch
that won't hold my arms,
or the legs of the race run
forwards, or the film
played backwards on his grandson's eyes.

Blackjack

1963;
we march.

I look out remedial
white windowed essays
from Pasadena
I will read tonight
and there you are visiting
three black sisters
excluded from official parade
'their skins unlovely.'

Orange and Fair Oaks
to grow on
to the stadium
blocks where you stand
silent; I am silent—

Nodding I say
'47 high noon in the bleachers,
Cards in town,
you jog the outfield grass
lagging loose balls,
how you lofted their cream-
skinned signatures
over the white heads
where we sat pigeontoed
circling their dugout,
how we carried your curled
name to our table
while your team cursed
your singed garters
on pennant flagged tongues.

As they saw nothing
but your teeth and eyes
we saw the jeering train
unwinding its sheets in Georgia,
your mail cringing with snake
juice spat in the Bronx;
and when you crossed
our borders we cheered
our black ace
of the marked deck of Westwood,
the bowl we stand in,
the counter where their salted
nuts stack in their vacuum cans.

We will not speak of broad
jumps over tracks,
yardlines of pigskin
jaunted, stitched white balls
spiked at your skull:
we will remember the found
sleep and meals you lost
running over bases
their pitchers feared covering,
balls you made them eat
now flowering from your son's
funeral car.

High blood pressure,
diabetes,
your eyes gone blind,
I will not answer.
I steel home
at your back

down the red clay road
of their stadium
recalling Rachel,
my own daughter,
on deck.

"Did he say Blackie?"
my brother said
of the white boy
in row G:
'Black Jack,
the gamble's taken,
the debt unpaid,
and the answer,
answered, still to come.'

Buck

I owe him for pictures
of champions I'd known,
or never seen,
or never known
and seen as men like
him, arched now
on a drunk
to ease arthritis,
his red tie
soaked in vomit,
his blue-ringed eyes
etched in glaucoma,
menace in serge-body
on his day off
near the cubicle
where he polishes
shoes, downtown
handballers at this Y.

Tomorrow
he will kneel
over the soft leather
of his polished nails,
his glasses pouched
as two black circles,
past years at sea,
his prison blindness,
concessions lost
to three promoters
the night Joe Louis
broke in the garden;
that he could box Sugar
in his prime,
hit like Archie,

teach Gavilan to bolo,
all this in signed
photos of his gallery,
is his hangover and cure
of the future of brushes.

Four bits,
he's changed men into boys
when they ask of his photos,
black and greased
in red velvet,
buckdancing in high-topped shoes,
he'll tell a lawyer
his two cushions
are his hero chamber;
'even with glasses off
I can tell you're a boy.'
He'll speak of his father
in Panama, lost and broken
in the canal
where ships cruise
to Frisco
keelhauling his shadow,
how he followed
his known sister
who'd died ironing
his suit cleaned
on her kitchen benches.

When my third son
died in intensive,
after early birth,
he took two photos
of his champions

for two sons I'd lost,
and signed their backs;
patting my shoulder
with mahogany nails
he called them grandsons,
turned toward two men
with black, unlaced shoes
patting their sleeping soles.

Alice Braxton Johnson

We lift your weight from chair
to bed to bedpan to chair to windowsill
as you stroke your way
from third floor infirmary windows
of our home;
I walk tearless to school
forgetting your name.

When you sit up all night
in your chair waiting for your children
to come, holding their ginwheel caravan
of parties, roughnecks following to beat
your son: trumpet-playing playboy Barrett
would call to the window in hazy
first light: "you there, Mom?";
and you always were.

So my mother nursed you over
years heart-stroked to the coalcar
of cemetery unnamed in my memory
but for the large kitchen where you reigned
hovering children, grandchildren plucked.
Your son, Barrett, would hold me loosening
in the '46 Ford from Rome to Brooklyn
breaking the limit—,
as he was to die leaving Rome
in the hazy morning ride
driven off the road
in a favor for a friend.

Did you save these roughnecks
who hated his laugh
when they rode him into the marked tree;
did you know he was to follow
you in his coalcar of our family?

I watch his black sole plant
his size twelve foot jamming
the gas, my eight-year-old hands
at his wheel, his fight with my mother
in mortgages, my mother's weight
on the seasoned floor of the moon,
the moon bleeding onto linoleum,
my father's face in the transom
where I was born, your house
torpedoed on my tearless walk to school,
and this chair empty.

Roland

—a tune of watchfulness—

They told me to sit on the highest stool,
eating ice cream to my grandfather's
beckoning, his hands batons of light,
knuckles chiseled in saving
his people without money.

Who waits for the watch that a white man
brought to our stoop some weeks after
his stitches healed, his eye put back
from the sidewalk glimmering with vision,
his wrecked car cleaned from the corner
where he stacked his flesh
put back by a black man from Canada?

'moments of your life
added years to mine'
the watch says to my son
named for the man who wove
the eye back in its socket,
who drew me from my mother
in the upstairs infirmary bedroom,
who pointed to my mole
marked for his father.

To the white man
interfaced on the streetcorner:
a toast from the highest stool
from whenever my son sits wheeling
in his own chair ticking;
and to Roland, to Roland,
this word from his seat
of ancestral force
on his feeding frequency
of the high mode.

Nightmare Begins Responsibility

I place these numbed wrists to the pane
watching white uniforms whisk over
him in the tube-kept
prison
fear what they will do in experiment
watch my gloved stickshifting gasolined hands
breathe *boxcar-information-please* infirmary tubes
distrusting white-pink mending paperthin
silkened end hairs, distrusting tubes
shrunk in his *trunk-skincapped*
shaven head, in thighs
distrusting-white-hands-picking-baboon-light
on this son who will not make his second night
of this wardstrewn intensive airpocket
where his father's asthmatic
hymns of *night-train,* train done gone
his mother can only know that he has flown
up into essential calm unseen corridor
going boxscarred home, *mamaborn, sweetsonchild*
gonedowntown into *researchtestingwarehousebatteryacid*
mama-son-done-gone/me telling her 'nother
train tonight, no music, no breathstroked
heartbeat in my infinite distrust of them:

and of my distrusting self
white-doctor-who-breathed-for-him-all-night
say it for two sons gone,
say nightmare, say it loud
panebreaking heartmadness:
nightmare begins responsibility.

Br'er Sterling and the Rocker

Any fool knows a Br'er in a rocker
is a boomerang incarnate; look at the blade
of the rocker, that wondrous crescent
rockin' in harness as poem.

To speak of poetry is the curled line straightened;
to speak of doubletalk, the tongue
gone pure, the stoic line a trestle
whistlin', a man a train comin' on:

Listen Br'er Sterling
steel-drivin' man, folk-said, folk-sayin',
that chair's a blues-harnessed star
turnin' on its earthy axis;

Miss Daisy, latch on that star's arc,
hold on sweet mama; Br'er Sterling's rocker glows.

Paul Laurence Dunbar: 1872–1906

One hundred years of headrags, bandages,
plantation tradition gone sour;
in the smokehouse, Newport, RI
a knotted metaphor collapsed in foyer,
Miss Ann finally understanding the elevator
where you sang your standard
imperfect lyrics.

Minstrel and mask:
a landscape of speech and body
burned in verbal space,
the match cinder unstandard:
double-conscious brother in the veil—
double-conscious brother in the veil:
double-conscious brother in the veil.

*—written on the 100th anniversary of his
birth, in continuum, in modality—Dayton, Ohio: 1972*

Gains

His voice soothes;
though his letters
are illegible
and unmailed
one gets the flow
from the trees
he describes,
or the uncle
who drank;
and when he died,
the uncle finer
than others of his
family, we must
believe the writer,
so I believe.

I see him on his gallery,
chinaball loping
in twilight, the old
folks telling
the dust as it settles
the night will be
cool, the humming insects
caressing bushes
blossoming like stars
named for women
on the slackened porch
in the weight of shoes
that stand open
to the dusky air.

How they speak are lines
in his books,
washed in the river never crossed,

or the tree whose shadow
roots underground,
or the chair that holds
an aunt who never walked
but raised his family,
her sky the sister
who faded as a voice
from the swamp
that packed her man
east of the small town
near the plantation
where you were born.

You come back home
to see tight arrows
of torn orchards
fruit-stubborn and thorned,
and you come back twice
to the river where the old
uncle talked, to bottles
stocked in *your* room
where the arms of his chair
cradled your stories
as they filled the air:
what is lost is his voice
in your voice; gained in
what you say and do.

No. 24

As you read your comics
she circles her left wrist,
thumb and forefinger,
nodding to friends;
your high voice caroms
in your coke bottle,
her alcohol stripping adhesive
from your gimpy knee;
though her fingers strike
matches on your fibrous biceps
it is waist, hips, thighs
she wears on frothy lips.

What of the centerfield wall?
She shrinks flammable
on your streaked uniform
where blood dries
on hipless pants.

Do not forget Birmingham:
we did not cry
but saw you shorten your open
stance for the hop
of eaten stitches:
Candlestick and Shea
your forelegs
broken in confetti.

Do not unhook your tongue-
broken grammar with commercials;
do not sell your restricted
billboard home secure.

Cup your hands
in familiar basket,
put your white suit
in her mitt
for she is there.
Her tubes stroke your evening
for the bat you wield:

she smiles with presents,
her wrists, fingers,
remembering what you were.
We fill your name in our space,
cokes and comics
on our shadowed wall.

Corrected Review

> 'The tree is unique, qualitatively speaking, and cannot be subject to purely
> quantitative comparison; it is impossible to reduce the world of
> sense-perceptions to quantitative categories. Qualitative things do not belong
> to matter, which is merely mirror for it, so it can be seen, but not so that it can
> be altogether limited to the material plane.'

> 'Man is created for the purpose of active participation in Divine Intellect, of
> which he is the central reflection.'

From the *source* comes the imagery and language,
compassion and complexity in the *one*
achieved in the imagination conjured,
admired in surrender and transcendence:
where is the *perfect* man?

Words beyond words to conjure this malaise
to infamy and death in effort
immanence forsaken:
to blow the music
maelstrom-tempered.

Our mode is our jam session
of tradition,
past in this present moment
articulated, blown through
with endurance,
an unreaching extended
improvised love of past masters,
instruments technically down:

structured renderings of reality
our final war with self;
rhetoric/parlance arena-word-consciousness:
morality: man to man
man to god
in a tree
more ancient than eden.

Alice

'The word made stone, the stone word'
'A RITE *is an action the very form of which is the result of a Divine
Revelation.'*

I

You stand waist-high in snakes
beating the weeds for the gravebed
a quarter mile from the nearest
relative, an open field in Florida: lost,
looking for Zora, and when she speaks
from her sunken chamber to call
you to her side, she calls
you her distant cousin, her sister
come to mark her burial place
with bright black stone.
She has known you would do this—
her crooked stick, her straight lick—
and the lie you would have to tell
to find her, and that you lied
to her relatives in a conjure-riddle
of the words you have uttered,
calling her to communion.

A black rock of ages you have placed
where there was no marker,
and though the snakes abound
in this preserve from ancestral space,
you have paid your homage
in traditional line, the face open:
your face in the woman-light of surrender
toughened in what you were.

II

Floods of truth flow from your limbs
of these pages in a vision swollen
in experience and pain:
that child you stepped into blossom
of a man's skull beaten into smile
of submission, you gathering horse nectar
for offering over a baby's crusted gasp,
for centuries of motherhood and atonement
for which you write, and the rite written.

And for this I say your name: Alice,
my grandmother's name, your name,
conjured in snake-infested field
where Zora Neale welcomed you home,
and where I speak from now
on higher ground of her risen
black marker where you have written
your name in hers, and in mine.

Part IV

from *Debridement*

> *When there is no history*
> *there is no metaphor;*
> *a blind nation in storm*
> *mauls its own harbors:*
> *spermwhale, Indian, Black,*
> *belted in these ruins.*

History as Cap'n Brown

"My name is John Brown; I have been well known as Old John Brown of Kansas. Two of my sons were killed here today, and I'm dying too. I came here to liberate slaves, and was to receive no reward. I have acted from a sense of duty, and am content to await my fate; but I think the crowd have treated me badly. I am an old man. Yesterday I could have killed whom I chose; but I had no desire to kill any person, and would not have killed a man had they not tried to kill me and my men. I could have sacked and burned the town, but did not; I have treated the persons whom I took as hostages kindly, and I appeal to them for the truth of what I say. If I had succeeded in running off slaves this time, I could have raised twenty times as many men as I have now, for a similar expedition. But I have failed."

The price of repression is greater than the cost of liberty.

Kansas and America

Some hated slavery
Some hated blacks
Some hated slaves
All loved land

The Music of Broadswords

We hacked them with broadswords:
our liquor dealer whose dive was the US court;
his brother-free-state-woman-baiter-bully;
our postmaster with no spit on his stamps;
our probate judge of warrants;
three slave-chasers who suckled their bloodhounds
in our muddy saloon: *Kansas*.

"Rescue Work": Dues

Crowns from the south:
black gold in a red box
marked "spleened";
black bottom hands locked
to riverboats at the wrists;
a Mexican serape staked
to a cottonplant with bowie knife;
patrollers near Lawrence,
Swamp of the Swans:
long-necked birds
in an eagle snare,
their feet, paddling, in cotton.

Dreams: American

At the rifle factory:
telegraph wires curl
in a one-horse wagon
taken where rivers
of blood wilt near
the armory gate—
60 rods more to the railroad
bridge towpath, making bullets—
my Lafayette sword,
wet powder, men
climbing into hillsides
of hostages we didn't kill;
screens of people we made
at the engine house we didn't use:
dead in the trestle work
in a moonless sky,
conspired in madness to steal
myself and steal away,
the mountaintop looks out,
its face the light
heartblow, a sword
upon the Golden Rule.

A scalp wound in a head rag
I pray out forty days
at the symbolic pallet:
put the insane in this pit,
dig to a subway pass:
the world is my family,
my brothers insane:
"insanity is like a very
pleasant dream to me."

Allegheny Shadows

The mountains call me
into arms of barricades,
its life-work
the economy-heart-
bloodbank in three phases:
black sloughs come after war
in English woolens;
black protection from duties,
cotton, ironworks, free trade;
black whirlwinds of gold
mushroom: industrial-
power-broker:
say we won't cooperate,
corner the market so we can circle
over our goods and bargain for ore.
Allegheny mountaintop:
an ensnared people on each fringe,
each settled, dollared ravine.

Plans

Railroad routes;
Indian territory;
southern Missouri:

Douglass believed in Brown
but not in his plan:
a secret page of mountain
to strawbrick and turpentine.

These are accounts payable:
hidden arms in an Ohio haymow,
hung by the heavens in scarlet
on Blue Ridge Mountain,
even as the black phalanx fails;
though I am sick with ague,
truth fevers that new-made grave,
one thousand pikes as stones.

Earthwork inspections
from Roman provinces
to Spanish chieftains:
Schamyl, Circassian,
Moina, Toussaint, Hugh Forbes.

Hot bloody spots
at watered points—
Potomac/Shenandoah:
I pledge my life to each slave,
with iron rather than in iron.

Reports: Kansas

Osawatomie Brown
killed by pro-slavery
man named White—
Frederick Brown is dead—
Brown hit by spent grape
canister, rifle shot—
killed by scalping
so bruised he didn't know
it 'til he reached the place:
with irons in hand I take
my scalp as Dred Scott
is taken in irons:

Come to the crusade:
blood is the issue,
not Negroes, *brothers.*

America Calls!

Called out of Egypt,
mother and ewe lamb
dead, the woods sunken
red men speckled,
their tongues
chained to a tree,
songs of black oak
keyed to scrotum:
what to survey with my tools:
round limbs of woman,
six sons, one daughter,
fevered insanities
of woman and child, dead,
on the mountain is my path.

Tending our newborn,
I walk the uneven woodpile
singing to child,
wife, through the day,
my step charmed by light
of woodshed. I carry her
three nights 'til she died.
Both died in their cradled arms.

One marries a girl
five years older than my oldest
as fate and promise of death
grow like trees burning,
my family these leaves
edged on two new-made graves:
action, one life to live:
spirits of my first woman
make me *do*
under Allegheny sky.

Though England kills my wool
as I sell it,
farm, racehorse, tannery,
surveyor: 1837: embargoes kill:
war kills my woolens,
love surveyed Oberlin
for black schools.

I raised six hundred
Saxony lambs
for my English masters,
saw it sold to my American
neighbor-friend-middleman:
quality wool for cheap factories;
cheap religion gone business
beats the slave
with an iron shovel.

I was born May Day;
my father stuttered.
In September, 1800,
Gabriel was born;
my father stuttered.

Clear songs of the Indian,
a chained blackened piglet
roasts on its chain,
I stutter at my own color-caste.

'Emperor': Shields Green: Fugitives

Sunday Meeting: *I b'lieve I'll go wid de ole man.*
At Chambersburgh Quarry:
I guess I'll go wid de ole man.
Black Monday: *I must go down to de ole man.*

Gen'l Tubman, as We Call Her

$10,000: dead or alive won't catch her;
dreamer of dreams and sickness will:

"Serpent in rocks and bushes,
head of a white-bearded old man,
then two younger heads spoke:
Come!
I was sick,
dreaming wishful deeds:
the heads spoke in tongues."

While at writing table
two wrens flew in
from their porch nest
fluttering attention;
a snake on our post
set to eat our young in the nest;

father killed the snake,
the wrens' songs burst
a successful omen.

Heads as flowers
not birds,
and cut off
to blossom
on a table:
then I heard of Harpers Ferry.

Four Worthies: Souls of Black Folk

To *Know*, in heart, in groin;
to *Move*, trestle, bog, boat, mask;
to *Love*, woman, child, land, trees;
to *Aspire*, where blood, sperm, bone join.

Fugitive Paths

Submit, fight, run:
young woman
demented in childbirth,
a boy four dead:
Turner 'live and dead;
Crandall's burned school
checkers our stacked churches,
Lovejoy murdered,
Fayette's stories of woe:

I swear a blood-feud
with slavery,
my sword of Gideon
amidst this vast veil:
"it is right for slaves
to kill their masters and escape."
Plans form their towpaths
to arsenal gates,
Gabriel's glory, openended.

Sambo's Mistakes: An Essay

Weaknesses:
> small good reading,
> thrown money on luxury—
> no capital;
> servility,
> talkativeness,
> disunity,
> sectarian bias:
> expects security with whites
> by tamely submitting to
> indignity, contempt, wrong.

Strengths:
> guns.

"S.P.W.": Journey of Consciousness

> These mountains are my plan:
> natural forts conceal
> armed squads of five
> on a twenty-five-mile line;
> slaves run off
> to keep them strong;
> the infirm underground,
> property insecure with blood:
> "Subterranean Pass Way"

"League of Gileadites": Messages

Nothing so charms the American
people as personal bravery:
Cinque on *Amistad,*
Lovejoy and Torrey:
all traitors must die.
Count on division among whites:
teach them
not to throw fire
in a wooden house—
lasso slave-catchers:
hold on to your weapons:
man-stealing is *rescue work.*

Sojourner Truth: Black Sybil in Salem

"Frederick, is God Dead?"

"No, and because God is not
dead, slavery can only end in blood."

Forty Days Looking Backwards: Notes from a Surveyor

Negro Steven found Kansas
after Indians found the land in themselves;
Kansas found: 1820—
slave barons leap into Missouri,
rape Mexico, Kansas-Nebraska Bill.

Free Soilers hate slaves not slavery.
Harpers Ferry sieves the Great Black Way.
In Waverly
I buried a son in thunderstorm
dead of cholera,
was refused food by rebels:
ploughed: planted corn,
fruit trees, vines,
hay for the stock:
fever and ague and guns
came 'cross the borders
glutting the polls:
I sought funds for arms.

At Big Springs some hated
slavery, more Negroes,
many slaves; the Indians were gone:
Kansas slave, Nebraska free:
Brooks broke Sumner's head
in Senate chambers
for telling these facts:
border ruffians rode Missouri
lines blanketed with killing.

We made our own "constructive
treason" at "Dutch Henry" settlement
in the Swamp of the Swan:
death by broadswords.

I took my instruments
into their camp
"sound on the goose"
mistook-mapmaker for slavery:
Owen, Frederick, Salmon, Oliver:
chain carriers, axman, marker.
One Georgian said:
"them damned Browns over there,
we're going to whip, drive out,
or kill, any way to
get shut of them, by God"
while I made entries
in my surveyor's book
to strike the blow.
The Wakarusa "treaty" put
federal troops in slave power,
armed bands at "Dutch Henry";
when ruffians warned our women
must leave, they burned two houses, a store,
and we sharpened our cutlasses.

"I am aware that you hold
my two sons, John and Jason,
prisoners—" I wrote
on scraps of paper that saved their lives.
Five sons built earthworks
in a circle near Lawrence;
beans, johnny-cake, mush,
milk, pumpkin, squash:
Kansas white only.

While they made out warrants
we camped near Osawatomie
while I had my visions from God:
slaughter at Osawatomie.
With little free-state support
we set out corn bread, meat,
blankets, running bullets,
utensils, loading,
came together at Black Jack
surrounded by a chain of forts,
patrollers in cavalry uniform.

I looked at the symmetry of heaven,
rolled dry beef, corn bread
bruised between stones,
in the ashes, felt the nervous power
of Ezra's affliction:
reports from thick chaparral
had me dead; we captured the cannon
'Sacramento,' joined Lane's
army at Nebraska City:
'No Quarter' was our motto.
The best battlement
is a well-armed guerrilla:
with an old wagon, cow,
a hidden slave, I slipped
through troops with surveyor tools,
disappearing from Kansas.

Jim Daniels: Hamilton Massacre: Parable

From Fort Scott I met Jim Daniels
selling brooms as disguise,
handsome mulatto; less than a year
ago eleven citizens were gathered up
by armed force under Hamilton,
formed in a line without trial,
and shot: all left dead, all free-staters:

What action has the president,
governors of Missouri, Kansas taken?

Daniels came to Osage settlement
from Missouri, wife, children,
another black man to be sold next day,
asking for help: *rescue work* in Missouri.

Posse to "enforce the law":
man-stealing, no; killing free-staters,
yes: look up the barrel of this shotgun,
see if you can find your slaves.

Plans: 2

I proposed a Negro school in Hudson: 1828;
in 1858 I fixed Harpers Ferry as spring
to the Great Black Way, central depots
spurred the Alleghenies, mountain arsenal:
pikes, scythes, muskets, shotguns,
Sharpes rifles for skilled officers:
Forbes betrayed us in temper, money:
we delayed a year in fever.

At Chatham we met,
'League of Freedom':
swamped marooned,
Appalachian range,
Indian territory,
the rout of Gabriel.
Rifle ball words
on rifle ball tongue:
most who gave arms
wanted use in Kansas only;
blacks hid me in Springfield,
rumors of scalping in Hartford,
cache of Harpers Ferry
in a guerrilla handbook:
I am through with Plymouth Rocks,
Bunker Hills, Charter Oaks,
Uncle Tom's Cabins:
those held accountable
are the mighty fallen.

I am without horses, holsters,
wagons, tents, saddles, bridles,
spurs, camp utensils, blankets,
intrenching tools, knapsacks,
spades, shovels, mattocks, crowbars,

no ammunition, no money
for freight or travel:
I have left my family poorly:
I will give my life for a slave
with a gun my secret passage.

'Manual for the Patriotic Volunteer'

Enough talk about bleeding Kansas.
Douglass could not be convinced,
his children were more interested,
Kagi, Richardson, Stevens, Moffett,
Shields Green: dead letters:
black laws of black dead
from Cincinnati to Canada.

"Odd Fellows": De Grass, McCune Smith,
Purvis, Vashon, Woodson, the Langstons,
Gen'l Tubman, Henson, Douglass,
Loguen, Payne, Ogden, Ward,
Garnet, Remond, Bibb: black heroes all.

"True Bands":
Delaney and Whitfield-Holly—
all my troops though they stay home.
Gen'l Tubman took sick,
visions of an iron weight broken:

We wrote our names on the hideout walls
hung by the heavens in blood:

Mountains and swamps are belts
to the Great Black Way,
Shenandoah to Loudoun Heights:
forays to the mountaintop.
Arms and ammunition lost advance-guard:
success was fifty men like Shields Green.

We gained entry with crowbar.
The eastbound B&O train arrived,
and was let go, carrying panic
to Virginia, Maryland, Washington:

passenger-strewn scraps of insurrection
sifted from the fleeing train;
it took eleven hours for our munitions
to move three miles;
Lee arrived with marines;
we did not bargain our hostages.
I arrived with ague,
fever, a secret
on a long string broken,
standing on a powder magazine.

The Meaning of Protest

Between the world and me
a black boy is a native
son with a long dream
if a white man will listen.
Uncle Tom's children
were eight men, all outsiders,
fish bellies living
underground.

Pagan Spain taught us the church
was woman as mystery, a penis
the sword to butcher each other;
Black Power! we're not going
to the moon, and in Bandung
white man can't come,
he's on a savage holiday.

Blossoms in a peanut field
won't bring me home;
something in the hum
of cotton is a glue
that won't hold red soil still;
twelve million voices spliced
on an iron cross
between the world, and me, and you.

Heartblow: Messages

I sit in cubbyhole,
wasp nests north and south,
woods to the west, ocean east,
the highway north a southern road.
Goggle-eyed lamplights
blink uneven wattage
as the pulses
of your soulful heart.

I met a man who gave you bread
and meat and a warm bed
while you wrote *Black Boy*,
another who shared your Chicago loft;
some wait for released papers,
some salve old photographs.

A campus librarian near
Hollywood reads the unread
books to move with Bigger,
sees Mary's spittle as sperm
pushing her trunk,
holds the body as you hack her neck,
watches Bessie's downdraft
as a cross-corner shot.

That parable of black man, white woman,
the man's penis slung to his shin,
erect, foaming in that woman's womb,
the ambivalent female with smirk-shriek,
daylights of coitus stuck together,
through the nights the razored solution;
that the black man is nature,
the woman, on her drilled pedestal, divine,
the man with razor an artisan

in symmetry steel and sharp blades—
let him melt into his vat of precious metal,
let the female wipe her face of sperm,
let the black man's penis shrink to normal
service, let the posse eat their whips instead.

On the Seine I thought of you
on the towpath to Notre Dame;
at the Blue Note looking for Bud
on his *parisian thorofare;*
caught your blues from black musicians
while you died alone in prose;
some said you'd died of disconnection;
souls said you dealt your own heartblow.

Afterword: A Film

'grandma's picket fence
balloon mask dancing
bloody moon your black ribcage.'

Erect in the movies
with a new job,
Trader Horn
and *The Gay Woman*
unfold in a twinbill:
drums, wild dancing,
naked men, the silver
veils on the South Side.
He imagines nothing:
it is all before him,
born in a dream:
a gorilla broke loose
from his zoo
in a tuxedo: baboon.
You pick your red bottom.
The Daltons are the movies.

On my wall are pictures:
Jack Johnson, Joe Louis,
Harlow and Rogers:
"see the white god and die."

Underground I live in veils,
brick and cement,
the confession beaten out,
slung with hung carcasses,
a bloody cleaver grunting,
a dead baby in the sewer:
"all the people I saw were guilty."

Marked black I was shot,
double-conscious brother in the veil—
without an image of act or thought
double-conscious brother in the veil—

The rape: "Mrs. Dalton, it's me,
Bigger, I've brought Miss Dalton
home and she's drunk":
to be the idea in these minds,
double-conscious brother in the veil—
father and leader where is my king,
veils of kingship will lead these folks
double-conscious brother in the veil—
"see the white gods and die"
double-conscious brother in the veil—

Debridement

Black men are oaks cut down.

*Congressional Medal of Honor Society
United States of America chartered by
Congress, August 14, 1958; this certifies
that* STAC John Henry Louis *is a member
of this society.*

*"Don't ask me anything about the
medal. I don't even know how I won
it."*

*Debridement: The cutting away of dead
or contaminated tissue from a wound
to prevent infection.*

America: love it or give it back.

Corktown

Groceries ring
in my intestines:
grits aint groceries
eggs aint poultry
Mona Lisa was a man:
waltzing in sawdust
I dream my card
has five holes in it,
up to twenty holes;
five shots out of seven
beneath the counter;
surrounded by detectives
pale ribbons of valor
my necklace of bullets
powdering the operating table.

Five impaled men loop their ribbons
'round my neck
listening to whispers of valor:
"Honey, what you cryin' 'bout?
You made it back."

Caves

Four M-48 tank platoons ambushed
near Dak To, two destroyed:
the Ho Chi Minh Trail boils,
half my platoon rockets
into stars near Cambodia,
foot soldiers dance from highland woods
taxing our burning half:

there were no caves for them to hide.

We saw no action,
eleven months twenty-two days
in our old tank
burning sixty feet away:
I watch them burn inside out:
hoisting through heavy crossfire,
hoisting over turret hatches,
hoisting my last burning man
alive to the ground,
our tank artillery shells explode
killing all inside:
hoisting blown burned squad
in tank's bladder,
plug leaks with cave blood:

there were no caves for them to hide—

In the Projects

Slung basketballs at Jeffries
House with some welfare kids
weaving in their figure eight hunger.

Mama asked if I was taking anything?
I rolled up my sleeves:
no tracks, mama:
"black-medal-man ain't street-poisoned,"
militants called:
"he's an electronic nigger!"

"Better keep electronic nigger 'way."
Electronic Nigger?
Mama, unplug me, please.

A White Friend Flies In from the Coast

Burned—black by birth,
burned—armed with .45,
burned—submachine gun,
burned—STAC hunted VC,
burned—killing 5–20,
burned—nobody know for sure;
burned—out of ammo,
burned—killed one with gun-stock,
burned—VC AK-47 jammed,
burned—killed faceless VC,
burned—over and over,
burned—STAC subdued by three men,
burned—three shots: morphine,
burned—tried killing prisoners,
burned—taken to Pleiku,
burned—held down, straitjacket,
burned—whites owe him, hear?
burned—I owe him, here.

Mama's Report

"Don't fight, honey,
don't let 'em catch you."

Tour over, gear packed,
hospital over, no job.

"Aw man, nothin' happened,"
explorer, altar boy—

Maybe it's 'cause they killed people
and don't know why they did?

My boy had color slides of dead people,
stacks of dead Vietnamese.

MP's asked if he'd been arrested
since discharge, what he'd been doin':

"Lookin' at slides,
lookin' at stacks of slides, mostly."

Fifteen minutes later a colonel called
from the Defense Department, said he'd won
                    the medal;

could he be in Washington with his family,
maybe he'd get a job now; he qualified.

The Democrats had lost, the president said;
there were signs of movement in Paris:

Fixing Certificates: Dog Tags: Letters Home

Our heliteam had mid-air blowout
dropping flares—5 burned alive.

The children carry hand
grenades to and from piss tubes.

Staring at tracer bullets
rice is the focal point of war.

On amphibious raid, our heliteam
found dead VC with maps of our compound.

On morning sick call you unzip;
before you piss you get a smear.

"VC reamed that *mustang* a new asshole"—
even at movies: "no round-eye pussy
no more"—

Tympanic membrane damage: high gone—
20–40 db loss mid-frequencies.

Scrub-typhus, malaria, dengue fever, cholera;
rotting buffalo, maggoted dog, decapped
children.

Bangkok: amber dust, watches, C-rations,
elephanthide billfolds, cameras, smack.

Sand&tinroof bunkers, 81/120 mm:
"Health record terminated this date by reason
of death."

Vacuolated amoeba, bacillary dysentery,
                    hookworm;
thorazine, tetracycline, darvon for diarrhea.

'*Conitus*': I wanna go home to mama;
Brown's mixture, ETH with codeine,
                    cortisone skin-creams.

Written on helipad fantail 600 bed *Repose;*
"no purple heart, hit by 'nother marine."

"Vascular repair, dissection, debridement":
sharp bone edges, mushy muscle, shrapnel:
                    stainless bucket.

Bodies in polyethylene bag: transport:
'Tan San Nhat Mortuary'

Blood, endotracheal tube, prep
abdomen, mid-chest to scrotum—

"While you're fixin' me doc,
can you fix them ingrown hairs on my face?"

"They didn't get my balls, did they?"
50 mg thorazine—"Yes they did, marine!"

Street-Poisoned

Swans loom on the playground
swooning in the basket air,
the nod of their bills
in open flight, open formation.
Street-poisoned, a gray mallard
skims into our courtyard with a bag:

And he poisons them—
And he poisons them—

Electronic-nigger-recruiter,
my pass is a blade
near the sternum
cutting in:
you can make this a career.

Patches itch on my chest and shoulders—
I powder them with phisohex
solution from an aerosol can:
you can make this a career.

Pickets of insulin dab the cloudy
hallways in a spray.
Circuits of change
march to an honor guard—
I am prancing:
I am prancing:

you can make this a career.

Makin' Jump Shots

He waltzes into the lane
'cross the free-throw line,
fakes a drive, pivots,
floats from the asphalt turf
in an arc of black light,
and sinks two into the chains.

One on one he fakes
down the main, passes
into the free lane
and hits the chains.

A sniff in the fallen air—
he stuffs it through the chains
riding high:
"traveling" someone calls—
and he laughs, stepping
to a silent beat, gliding
as he sinks two into the chains.

Debridement: Operation Harvest Moon: *On Repose*

The sestina traces a circle in language and body.

Stab incision below nipple,
left side; insert large chest tube;
sew to skin, right side;
catch blood from tube
in gallon drain bottle.
Wash abdomen with phisohex;
shave; spray brown iodine prep.

Stab incision below sternum
to symphis pubis;
catch blood left side;
sever reddish brown spleen
cut in half; tie off blood supply;
check retroperitoneal,
kidney, renal artery bleeding.

Dissect lateral wall
abdominal cavity; locate kidney;
pack colon, small intestine;
cut kidney; suture closely;
inch by inch check bladder,
liver, abdominal wall, stomach:
25 units blood, pressure down.

Venous pressure: 8; lumbar
musculature, lower spinal column
pulverized; ligate blood vessels,
right forearm; trim meat, bone ends;
tourniquet above fracture, left arm;
urine, negative: 4 hours; pressure
unstable; remove shrapnel flecks.

Roll on stomach; 35 units blood;
pressure zero; insert plastic blood
containers, pressure cuffs; pump chest
drainage tube; wash wounds sterile
saline; dress six-inch ace wraps;
wrap both legs, toe to groin; left arm
plaster, finger to shoulder: 40 units blood.

Pressure, pulse, respiration up;
remove bloody gowns; scrub; redrape;
5 cc vitamin K; thorazine: sixth
laparotomy; check hyperventilation;
stab right side incision below nipple;
insert large chest tube; catch blood drain bottle . . .

The Family of Debridement

Theory: Inconvenienced subject will return to hospital
if loaned Thunderbird
Withdrawn. Hope: Subject returns,
Treatment:
Foreclosure for nine months unpaid mortgage;
wife tells subject hospital wants deposit,
Diseased cyst removal:
'Ain't you gonna give me a little kiss good-bye'
Subject-wife: To return with robe and curlers—
Subject tells friend he'll pay $15 to F's stepfather
if he'll drive him to pick up money owed him.

"This guy lives down the street,
I don't want him to see me coming."

'It looked odd for a car filled with blacks
to be parked in the dark in a white neighborhood,
so we pulled the car out under a streetlight
so everybody could see us."

Store manager: "I first hit him with two bullets
so I pulled the trigger until my gun was empty."

"I'm going to kill you, you white MF*," store manager*
told police. Police took carload, F and F's parents for
further questioning. Subject died on operating table: 5 hrs:

Subject buried on grass slope, 200 yards
east of Kennedy Memorial,
overlooking Potomac and Pentagon,
to the south,
Arlington National Cemetery.

Army honor guard
in dress blues,
carried out assignment
with precision:

Part V

from *Song: I Want a Witness*

to sing is to speak immediately
of the transcendent

Don't Explain

Song: *I Want a Witness*

Blacks in frame houses
call to the helicopters,
their antlered arms
spinning; jeeps pad
these glass-studded streets;
on this hill are tanks painted gold.

Our children sing
spirituals of *Motown*,
idioms these streets suckled
on a southern road.
This scene is about power,
terror, producing
love and pain and pathology;
in an army of white dust,
blacks here to *testify*
and *testify*, and *testify*,
and *redeem*, and *redeem*,
in black smoke coming,
as they wave their arms,
as they wave their tongues.

Kneading

She kneads the kernels, grains,
powder of the filled containers,
and makes the bread that fuses
my sons and the world of the house,
and the dust is a resin of her face,
and she is kneading again.

With a scar shaped like an anchor,
an inch-long break at the wrist
where she hammered the window jamb,
and the soft belly of my own furred
animals, these sons quiver in the shadows
of her dress, faced into the crevices
of her tenderness, and the kneading.

The two absent boys who linger in the bread
of the kneading hands, in the eyes
and ears of the mother, kneading,
go, back and forth, with their real
brothers, hitching themselves to these germs;
and their father chews the meat
that passes into their mouths,
these juices from kneading, these gums
torn with the teeth of death, the death
of those like them, living, and eating
this kneaded bread, their mother's
and their father's kneading, this meat.

The Drive In

I drive west from the old dump,
ice booming, its layers
glistening patterns
in the minus air,
trees cracking under a load of ice.

The mink on the passenger floor,
who had quivered near the car door,
chased by dogs and snowmobiles,
unable to run in the high snow,
unable to feed in the ruddered woods,
stiffens on an old magazine.

I see a pelt and some food for a dog;
my VW made from war weaves
over the drifting snow; taken up
by the tail the mink's eyes widen,
headlights dimming in the high snow,
sounds of cracking ice booming—
sounds of driven, ruddered snow—

Herring Run

Herring run
in the silver morning
among the thudding;
forty boys with flippers
and sticks thump
the planet water
and the scoop
of the fish
is the thumping.
Ninety miles from New York
this converted estate
from the New Deal,
the emotionally disturbed
roam over the grounds
and in the water
hunt in the spring run.

A boy named Melvin,
who'd kicked a hole in ice
last winter and refused to come out,
and a boy named Hicks
flit in the country air,
ax and hunting knife,
as the herring puff
on the banksides still running.

Lunch break and their drugs,
and they are calm;
enrichment to make them write;
night check to make them sleep.

At age ten
with a bottle of Scotch
and a conga drum
an emotionally disturbed
boy drums on the *A* train
between 125th and 59th Street,
panhandling herringbone blues.

Now in runs on the capitol bank
they think blacks
are a brand of cracker;
herring don't run anymore.

Continuous Visit

Your canoe stops
near a sunflower patch
where your daughters
swim in two weedy ditches
off our shaky docks,
cast frogs, hooked through
their mouths,
bass not yet biting.

Moose pie, creamed
beans and Jell-O
opt new appetites,
your girls beach
sandpiled in towels;
under forty oaks
you read chronicles
from typed peach paper,
last year's spirits
pitched in its threshing,
blood from the suture
of my family.

This suture is race
as it is blood,
long as the frozen
lake building messages
on typewritten paper,
faces of my ancestors,
warm in winter only
as their long scars touch ours.

Dead Oaks

I eat on all fours
over the dank hole
where my 200-year-
old oak once was
now in a pile at
the cord-wound corral.
I think of the smell
of this earth,
earth that poisons
this brimmed cemetery,
burial ground
long since forgotten.

On a farm in the eastern
half of this state,
an old woman sat
on her porch whistling
an Indian tune
though whittling
in Norwegian.

I listen to her son
sing of the death of his
brother in war,
his brothers dying
in the old ancestral
earth of the Far East
or in African mines
plaqued in its gold
to our commercial hearth.

I chop at the tree
to make kindling
as the fire arches

out of sight, food
in this old place, this hole
in the cosmic earth.

Pale in his death heat,
the son of the mother
on the porch, having
heard of her death,
reading of his brother's
death, reading of the death
of his brothers:
Indian, Norwegian,
sits on this old stump
and whittles, whistling:
congress of the last
poetic word, this damp
ceremonial hill, this oak.

Oak

She lifts the two boys on
the overturned rowboat, a galley
plank as a slide;
gummy paint on the underside
sticks to their shoes;
as they walk the eggshell
white blackens the swaying birch boat.

She lifts cracked plaster,
glass, rock from the foundation,
hunting for nails, her pigtailed
sway the break of oars
beating the lake overturned;
she works for new grass
that springs up, the three oaks
burned to death in winter,
mistook victims of our rubbish pile.
A hundred-gallon garbage can
freezes in its burned tracks;
a wire cylinder holds our burned
paper; near the chain fence
we chew the burned oak
with a two-man saw.

In the attic is an old bed;
I hear its thumping as I watch her
leafing seeds to the hoed land
in foot-deep holes in our thawing ground,
trees that must grow in gravel.

We begin to live in the old way:
fertile eggs in a poaching tin,
cooked meal, kneaded bread rising
on the open-air rack,
stumps at our garden table.

As the spring thaws she plants,
uncovers, hoes, digs for the rich
earth; in gravel we take up the saw;
in the old way we cut dead oak.

Breaded Meat, Breaded Hands

The heat of the oven
glazed on the windowed
doors, the percolated lines
of water drizzle down;
she cooks over the heated
fires in a blaze of meat.

The shelled pan-baked peanuts
ground to a paste
pass over the chicken
ripped off by tornadoes.

Raisins of my son's eyes
garnish the pork loin,
kidneys and beef heart.

In the corner the rock salt
and the crushed snow
churn the coconut
ice cream, vanilla
beans and two half pints
of cream atop the thundering
washing machine.

Boards thick with sweet potatoes,
the piecrust cooled in the icebox,
dough souring on the stove top,
the hands of our children
damp with flour and butter
of their burning skins,
and the marks of cooking,
churnings of the heated kitchen.

Yogurt to cover the cucumbers,
sautéed onions, the curd of some

cabbaged blood wine, bottled
vinegar which tastes like olive oil.

At the hearth of this house,
my woman, cutting the bits of guile,
the herbs of warmth she has butchered
into the pots,
the pans of grease
that feed this room, and our children,
condensed in the opaque room—
the hearth of this house
is this woman, the strength of the bread
in her hands, the meat in her marrow
and of her blood.

Lathe: Shirl's Tree

I sit at my lathe
since she loves trees,
covered with ash or maple:
ash beautiful
as this burn my chisel
makes in her grain
from large and small crevice
as a wood
gauges its fibers,
only a pocket of child.

This hard New England cherry
is the same dry.
Linseed and turpentine on a rag
make the wood,
make my lathe
roll in her oiled fibers:
well-wrought pocket of child:
ashen and cherry-oiled tree.

Last Affair: Bessie's Blues Song

Disarticulated
arm torn out,
large veins cross
her shoulder intact,
her tourniquet
her blood in all-white big bands:

Can't you see
what love and heartache's done to me
I'm not the same as I used to be
this is my last affair

Mail truck or parked car
in the fast lane,
afloat at forty-three
on a Mississippi road,
Two-hundred-pound muscle on her ham bone,
'nother nigger dead 'fore noon:

Can't you see
what love and heartache's done to me
I'm not the same as I used to be
this is my last affair

Fifty-dollar record
cut the vein in her neck,
fool about her money
toll her black train wreck,
white press missed her fun'ral
in the same stacked deck:

Can't you see
what love and heartache's done to me
I'm not the same as I used to be
this is my last affair

Loved a little blackbird
heard she could sing,
Martha in her vineyard
pestle in her spring,
Bessie had a bad mouth
made my chimes ring:

Can't you see
what love and heartache's done to me
I'm not the same as I used to be
this is my last affair

Homage to the New World

Surrounded by scientists in a faculty
house, the trees wet with hot rain,
grass thickening under the trees,
welcomers come, ones and twos,
gifts of shoehorns, soap, combs,
half a subscription to the courier,
some news about changing
plates, the nearest market,
how to pick up the trash, a gallon
of milk twice a week, OK?

On the third day here,
a friend came in the night to announce
a phone call and a message,
and heard the shell go in
and the rifle cocking,
our next-door animal-vet neighbor,
and cried out, "Don't shoot,"
and walked away to remember the phone
and the message, the crickets,
and the rifle cocking,
grass and hot rain.

I write in the night air
of the music of Coltrane,
the disc of his voice in this
contralto heart, my wife;
so what! Kind of Blue,
these fatherless whites
come to consciousness
with a history of the gun—
the New World, if misery had
a voice, would be a rifle cocking.

The Negatives

She agitates
the quart developing tank
in total darkness,
our windowless bath;
the cylinder slides
inside against the film
for ten minutes
at 70 degrees.
I can see the developer
acid in the luminous
dial of my watch:
she adds the stop-bath.
The hypo fix
fastens the images
hardening against light
on her film and papers.
I imagine her movement
at night as her teeth grind:
I know she dreams the negatives.

Photographs

Felt negatives work the pores
coal black in darkness
double negatives;
now in the light
the emulsive side down
on top of brown-gray paper
human images rise.

From bath to workbench
in our tarpaper shack;
stacks of grade paper appear,
fixed images on archival prints;
tempered, the controlled chemicals
edge 'round the contact sheet
edged in a family grave.

Print and stir dektol
on agfa brovira bromide paper,
apply stop action, keep moving
saline amniotic fluid,
dilute with hot water.

The iron water cools;
paper shown to light
turns black
as skin on my arm.

The Night of Frost

I walk out in the first
autumn frost over dog
dung, puddin' rock, acorns,
gutted pumpkin, to the last
three letters on the mailbox
at the road; I paste my decals
over the owner's name
as I pull the lid
and stare in.

I walk on the squat rock fence
to our apple tree,
then near the trailer
across the road
where a cyclops woman
with glaucoma
bends in nightclothes
watering her plants.

I walk back over her sold
stone peering at her old house,
the crooked clabbered sidings,
uneven cut windowjams,
slatted tarpaper roof,
cut and hammered into scars.

I walk as negative
image over white crusted
grave stones as my dark feet
stamp their footprints.

Utility Room

She shades the prints bathed
in what iron water there is,
artesian iron spring water;
pictures of winter green
blue in darkness,
the second hand stops.

She shakes the developing tank
as a uterus
mixing developer
to the negatives
where no light appears;
I hold her hips
as saline and acid
pock up images.
I see my children
of these negatives
in a windowless room.

A simple enlarger,
a bulb with a shade,
images born through her lens
packed on the contact sheet;
fatted negatives under thick
condenser glass,
prints from her uterus,
cramps from her developing tank.

At the Cemetery

1.
Horton, Smith,
Rose, are the landmarks:
Horton the whaler
turned to farming
to sell to the markets,
a nearby street bears
his clan;
the road is Smith,
who rolled two horsedrawn
wagons filled with boulders
from Plymouth Rock;
the weathercock etched
in Rose tells directions
on a wooden staff
at the road's edge.

This house is a *Horton*
house, the addition *Rose,*
1830; my sons pedal
in the brimming sand:
Smith, Horton, Rose.

2.
They cut to the center,
veer to the apple tree
on this northern border
of the tree line.

A great apple tree
lies on this northern
boundary, its bruised
fruit dropping like flares
among the puddin' stone;

as they climb the tree
their photographs
blacken in their acid
as if burnt by sunlight,
the corners etch and turn up
in their light brimming curls.

Spent birch treelimbs
leave diamond shapes
where the limbs once grew;
they stride in these meters
up the burst limbs,
their feet in diamond
shapes where the limbs were.
I hear the roots underground
turn nosedown
away from bones
toward the artesian line
much much below.

The Borning Room

I stand in moonlight
in our borning room,
now a room of closets
changed by the owners.
Once only the old
and newborn slept
on this first floor,
this boarded door
closed now to the hearth
of our wood burning.

I look over the large bed
at the shape of my woman;
there is no image
for her, no place
for the spring child.
Her cornered shape dreams
a green robed daughter
warmed in a bent room
close to fireplace oven,
warmed by an apple tree:
the old tried to make it new,
the new old; we will not die here.

The Families Album

Goggled mother with her children
stomp on the tar road,
their dresses black:
sugar maple, white pine,
apple tree, sumac,
young birch, red oak,
pine, cedar, deer moss
watch the archival print
in their death march,
for they lived here,
as they live with us now,
in these slanted pine floors
they tried to straighten,
in these squared windows
unsquared, in wallpaper torn
down, in the bare beams
of the addition plastered,
in a mother's covered eye
diseased by too much light,
too much blood which struck
her husband dead, too much
weed to makethe farm work,
too many crooked doorways
on a dirt road tarred over.

This old house which was hers
made her crooked back a shingle,
her covered eye this fireplace oven,
her arms the young pine beams
now our clapboard siding;
the covered well runs in this dirt
basement, her spring watering her grave
where the fruit, vegetables, woodpile, lie.

Trays: A Portfolio

1.
At the tray
she looks in the heart
of these negatives,
her borning room
fireplace oven full of pitch,
roasting the brick sidings,
her heart warmed
from the inside cradle
in a windowless bath.

2.
Two African veils
on two sons
clothed in their isolettes
burn in a hospital.

3.
From a pan of chemicals
the images turn from black
to white flames as we
agitate the quart
tank developer:
black men,
two sons stoppered
from isolette
to incinerator,
a child walks
under her apron
as film develops
in her black and white eyes;
she stoops over the boys
on the primed cut smock,
born, inflated, enlarged.

4.

We grade paper from one to six
as our number of children;
little contrast to extreme contrast,
two to four the perfect negative
in our perfect family
enlarged as a light bulb
with a shade; we fight
the dirt on the negatives,
touch up with spotting liquid
absorbed by numbered paper:
contact: print:
blacken our negatives with light.

5.

Pumpkin, squash, green
peppers, onions, carrots,
squat in cellar piles;
I hear the gargle
of hot water pipes
gushing through copper;
the mice spin between walls
eating paper under my drain;
the waterpump whirs
iron rust in each drain
from artesian fields underground.
From the cellar door
near the boarded well
is a concord grape arbor;
I walk by evergreen seedlings,
verbena bush
looking for cranberries
to harvest as drops of blood
on a weedeaten farm.

In a clot of pines
my sons roll in their bog
in a pool of grass,
each step trundled,
each laugh bedded with blood.

History as Apple Tree

Cocumscussoc is my village,
the western arm of Narragansett
Bay; Canonicus chief sachem;
black men escape into his tribe.

How does patent not breed heresy?
Williams came to my chief
for his tract of land,
hunted by mad Puritans,
founded Providence Plantation;
Seekonk where he lost
first harvest, building, plant,
then the bay from these natives:
he set up trade.
With Winthrop he bought
an island, *Prudence;*
two other, *Hope* and *Patience*
he named, though small.
His trading post at the cove;
Smith's at another close by.
We walk the Pequot trail
as artery or spring.

Wampanoags, Cowesets,
Nipmucks, Niantics,
came by canoe for the games;
matted bats, a goal line,
a deerskin filled with moss:
lacrosse. They danced;
we are told they gambled their souls.

In your apple orchard
legend conjures Williams' name;
he was an apple tree.
Buried on his own lot
off Benefit Street
a giant apple tree grew;
two hundred years later,
when the grave was opened,
dust and root grew
in his human skeleton:
bones became apple tree.

As black man I steal away
in the night to the apple tree,
place my arm in the rich grave,
black sachem on a family plot,
take up a chunk of apple root,
let it become my skeleton,
become my own myth:
my arm the historical branch,
my name the bruised fruit,
black human photograph: apple tree.

Part VI

from History Is Your Own Heartbeat

Blue Ruth: America

I am telling you this:
the tubes in your nose,
in the esophagus,
in the stomach;
the small balloon
attached to its end
is your bleeding gullet;
yellow in the canned
sunshine of gauze,
stitching, bedsores,
each tactoe cut
sewn back
is America:
I am telling you this:
history is your own heartbeat.

The Dark Way Home: Survivors

Married to rural goldmines
in southern Minnesota,
your money is land, horses,
cows all of metal:
the area is German;
the religion Gothic, acute,
permanent, in white heat
and telephone wires;
you live with a family where
each issue is food,
where word is appetite
you hunger in: hunting
your slough for teal;
beating your sons with machinery
and your oiled might;
setting your chickens to peck
your children; roping them homegrown
to the tractors and cuckleburs,
giving them no private thoughts
but rebellion:

fish and hunt for surplus
acreage to corncrib you up,
lutheran or catholic
in taste and ambition;
love grandchildren,
love potatoes,
love beans, love venison,
love pheasant, love berries,
love bass, love rocks
become fossils, love sweetcorn,
shucked in guts, silently
burrowing what grows
but can't love, burgeoning,
lovely, like this.

Love Medley: Patrice Cuchulain

"Stirrups, leggings, a stainless
steel slide, a dishpan, sheet,
a thread spool, scissors,
three facemasks, smocks, paper
overshoes, a two-way mirror, dials":
the head and left arm
cruise out, almost together,
and you drop into gloves,
your own ointment
pulling your legs
binding your cord; the cheesed
surface skin, your dark
hairless complexion, the metallic room,
orchestrate and blow up your lungs,
clogged on protein and vitamins,
for the sterile whine of the delivery
room and your staff of attendants.
It is free exercise when the cord's
cut; you weigh in for the clean up
as your mother gets her local
for her stitches: boy, 6 lbs 13 oz.

As you breathe easily, your mother's
mother is tubed and strapped,
hemorrhaging slowly from her varices;
your two dead brothers who could
not breathe are berries
gone to rot at our table:
what is birth but death
with complexity: blood, veins,
machinery and love: our names.

Good Samaritan Hospital

'Point It Out, Point It Out to Me'

The story goes: wide purple
eyes woven in sugar, we add
some vinegar and hot dye;
the non-toxic drip of our
continent on inhabitants
is odorless as lightning;
we hug the tributaries
to our skin of tobacco—
the cotton crop perfectly dry;
the drink is cane sugar
which yeasts on the docks,
the blue-black molasses
shucked and popped in the oven.

The best trained cooks
are the best trained spies
who shift the vats where the lab
learns more about blood sugar
and hemoglobin—
black and white ice cream
bins pucker this sexual
imagery; the rarest blood
rose is skinned by white hands;
a garden is a white woman
with a penchant for tropical flowers.
What is the smell of black semen
stuck in white wombs
in 1876 when the troops withdraw?

We explore the illiterate halls
with a photographic eye;
the flick we've made is our bible
for which there's no cost;
we splice in our parts,
"The Birth of a Nation,"
a wide angle close-up,
buck, posse, a good horse.

Lovely's Daughters: Visitors

We packed our cuts
and insect bites with rich damp earth.

The breeze swung our own birches
in clots of music.

We ate the tangled punch grapes,
crushed brown bodies in vines.

4-inch nails snagged our blankets,
gowned on the treehouse stair,

bats flew, tangling our hair;
we danced with the spider crayfish.

Naked, on the hot night road,
we squashed fireflies on our chests
as they burned;

fallen corn, haymow, cuckleburs,
the unplowed rocks, hail,
swollen tornadoes cracking

our bedwater;
these centigrade nights
we cuddle our stink to keep warm.

The bees circling,
blood down our legs,
we stuffed soybean leaves in us.

Now we swell in the visitor cove
in the fifth floor scissor-light,
punctured bells on a rope
twenty feet from your door,
six portwind odors
staved in the toxic night;
your grandchildren grow
taut as sandpaper in your
pregnant daughters—one
in serape, one in wood shoes—
we switch the wheelchair
between us, witnesses sworn
under oath, music our own heartbeats,
digging our poetry with our nails.

Clan Meeting: Births and Nations: A Blood Song

We reconstruct lives in the intensive
care unit, pieced together in a buffet
dinner: two widows with cancerous breasts
in their balled hands; a 30-year-old man
in a three-month coma
from a Buick and a brick wall;
a woman who bleeds off and on from her gullet;
a prominent socialite, our own nurse,
shrieking for twins, "her bump gone";
the gallery of veterans, succored,
awake, without valves, some lungs gone.

Splicing the meats with fluids
seasoned on the dressing room
table, she sings "the bump gone"
refrain in this 69-degree oven,
unstuffing her twin yolks
carved from the breast, the dark meat
wrapped in tinfoil and clean newspaper;
the half black registered nurse
hums her six years in an orphanage,
her adopted white family,
breaded and primed in a posse,
rising in clan for their dinner.

We reload our brains as the cameras,
the film overexposed
in the x-ray light,
locked with our double door
light meters: race and sex
spooled and rung in a hobby;
we take our bundle and go home.

This Is My Son's Song: *"Ungie, Hi Ungie"*

A two-year-old boy
is a blossom in the intensive
care aisle, small as
a ball-bearing,
round, open and smooth;
for a month, in his first
premature hours, his shaved
head made him a mohawk Indian
child, tubes the herbs
for his nest, a collapsed lung
the bulbous wing of a hawk.
Slivered into each sole
is an intravenous solution
to balance his losses
or what they take out
for the lab; the blue spot
on his spine is a birth
mark of needle readings;
the hardened thighs immune
from 70 shots of various
drugs of uneven depth; the chest
is thick with congestion: bad
air and mucus—good air and pure
oxygen; jerky pouch buffalo lungs—
It does not surprise me
when he waits patiently for his
grandmother, over her five-hour
painless operation; he has
waited in his isolette
before: the glow in his eyes
is for himself, will and love:
an exclamation of your name:
"Ungie, hi Ungie"; you are saved.

Sack 'A Woe: Gallstones as History

One's still in, a goose egg's
made its own bile duct;
the 120 wound pearls
season before doctors,
diamonds to be sorted,
etched in pancreas juice;
they photograph this collection
of off-color radishes,
milky and boiled,
for the medical museum.

A gallstone's seed is berry
wild in fuzz, boned
and filleted, cured,
for each special attack.

So many transfusions
have seeded in sediment
the antibodies won't be identified;
a pint of O blood,
pickles from the lab,
a miraculous find;
they pick the unetherized
weedbeds of tissue and stone
for leaks or obstructions;
cut you like mush melon
suckled in worms
picking your liver
and gall bladder
the color of squash.
Jaundice was your tenth
year on the farm;
five conscious hours
they pickax inside;
you float down this aisle
boxed, fingered, eyed.

History as Bandages: Polka Dots and Moonbeams

One is an igloo
of whalebone and oil
and a poisonous gas;
one is a canoe under water
laden with wild rice,
grubs, and Indian arrows;
one is a banjo
packed with thin dirt
in Richmond, Virginia:
Gabriel: 1800;
one is a round bubble
of mustard rock
broken on an Indian squaw;
one is a print of a buffalo,
bearded, masked, made
musty skinned hair.

The white rectangular
patchwork covers all these
national wounds kept
secretly bound, at night,
absorbing color and blood and bones
of all shapes and disguises.

One Lives, One Dies: Both/And: A Choice of Colors

Wild rice grows along the banks
of your house, stilted
and holding you up;
your gowned daughters squeeze
pimples and curls and magpie
around the kitchen, ironing
and rinsing their mouths—
bass after minnows and frogs;
you think of the twin-grained
children in the intensive care
unit, and their parents,
race-hate, musical machines
that tear at your stitches,
the leadfilling gas from the trucks,
butchers in green smocks
and your own life in the wick
of Christmas pine and pheasants:
almost completely gutted, you count
your three mixed fledglings:
Roland, Stephen, Patrice;
seed, pollen, pine.

24th Avenue: City of Roses: Anesthesia: 2

You sit, puckered and dry,
on a wicker chair on our porch;
the roses and oaks enclose you in
mists of blossoms and garden
vegetables in your own yard;
sloughs of children are mallards,
your grandson a black and tan goose
with no neck and loose hair,
a pugged bill, unafraid,
who has pulled you back
from death with his own
voice: *"hi Ungie, Hi."*

I think of the phosphates
that gurgle in the drains
of your eyes, the salts
and vitamins, a stacked deck
on a seven-foot shelf,
baked dishes burnished in tubes
of fine print
surrounding the breakfast nook;
sometimes sulphur won't mix
with your thin blood,
you yellow into a spacious bug,
bloom for six hours, nap
or sew or read nursery-
song patter to sprout at our table.
Yellow again as your liver
shrinks to normal size,
nocturnal buds fusing to rend,
your eyes jelly and slim
in the evening porchlight,
go out in sudden pain,
rekindle, electric as smoke;
we fire our thermostat
measuring your meal and toilet.

Here Where Coltrane Is

Soul and race
are private dominions,
memories and modal
songs, a tenor blossoming,
which would paint suffering
a clear color but is not in
this Victorian house
without oil in zero degree
weather and a forty-mile-an-hour wind;
it is all a well-knit family:
a love supreme.
Oak leaves pile up on walkway
and steps, catholic as apples
in a special mist of clear white
children who love my children.
I play "Alabama"
on a warped record player
skipping the scratches
on your faces over the fibrous
conical hairs of plastic
under the wooden floors.

Dreaming on a train from New York
to Philly, you hand out six
notes which become an anthem
to our memories of you:
oak, birch, maple,
apple, cocoa, rubber.
For this reason Martin is dead;
for this reason Malcolm is dead;
for this reason Coltrane is dead;
in the eyes of my first son are the browns
of these men and their music.

Martin's Blues

He came apart in the open,
the slow motion cameras
falling quickly
neither alive nor kicking;
stone blind dead
on the balcony
that old melody
etched his black lips
in a pruned echo:
We shall overcome
some day—
Yes we did!
Yes we did!

Madimba

Music is its own heartbeat

Double-conscious sister in the veil,
Double-conscious sister in the veil;
Double-conscious sister in the veil:
Double-conscious sister in the veil.

You beat out the pulse with your mallets,
the brown wishbone anemones
unflowered and unworn in Chicago congo
prints, images, otherness, images

from the fossilbank: Madimba.
Black Man; I'm a black man; black—
A-um-ni-pad-me-hum—
another brother gone:

"the first act of liberation
is to destroy one's cage"—
a love supreme;
a love supreme.

Images: words: language
typing the round forms: Juneteenth,
baby, we free, free at last:
black man, I'm a black man.

A garden is a manmade vision,
rectangular, weeded, shelled,
pathed, hosed, packed in,
covered with manure, pruned;

I own you; you're mine, you
mine, baby: to bear unborn things.
Double-conscious sister in the veil:
Double-conscious sister in the veil.

Black woman: America is artful
outside time, ideal outside space;
you its only machine: Madimba:
Double-conscious sister in the veil.

Come Back Blues

I count black-lipped
children along river-creek,
skimming between bog,
floating garbage
logs, glistening tipped
twilight and night beaks;
the drowned drown again
while their parents
picket the old library and pool
special fish
taken up in poison—
you've come back
to count bodies again
in your own backyard.

Time for Tyner: Folksong

The medley goes like this:
We sit in a bar in a draft
from the swinging door as
some patrons leave in wings
which are fleecelined coats
echoing with the ice cream
red of the police pick-up van;
an African instrument is not
the piano; an African village
is not the Both/And; an African
waltz is not in 3/4.

It strikes me in his juice
is the love of melody;
he thumbs the solo piano
in a wickerchair blues
tripping a rung tune in its
scratching black keys
shimmering in the plant light:
we are all covered green.

It is a political evening:
posters of Mingus and Trane,
recordings of Bud Powell,
Bird under false names,
the economy of Miles;
I take it in scratchpad
English in the waxed light
as his liner notes pucker
on our lips in this country
abiding and earless.

The Dance of the Elephants

Part I

The trains ran through the eleven
nights it took to vacate the town;
relatives and lovers tacked in a row
on the button-board sidings,
wails of children tossed in a pile
wails of women tossed in a salad
to be eaten with soap and a rinse.
Those who took all they had to the borders,
those who took their bottles
three centuries old, those who
thought only of language, the written
word, are forgiven.
One daughter is riding on the train
above her mother, above her mother,
into the tunnel of the elephants.

Culture tells us most about its animals
singing our children asleep, or let them
slip into a room as smoothly as
refrigeration.

Part II

To be comforted by Swiss music
is a toy elephant in a box,
skimming the nickelplated air.
Beethoven's a passion dance
forgotten in a stamped coin—
it is magic—it is magic—

We dance the old beast round the fireplace,
coal engines fuming in a row,
elephant chimes in a toy rain—
human breath skimming the air.

We skim the air—
it is magic—the engines
smelling the chimes,
Beethoven chiming the magic—
we escape it on a train.

Sung in America,
the song some telescopic sight,
a nickelplated cream,
a small girl cuddles her elephant,
the song in the streets
leaping the train windows,
and what love as the elephant chimes.

Mission

Weeds are in her face
she skates in 20-below
thin air skipping the risen
pockets of lake ice
moving with urgency
in her dance—
we have swept an icerink
in a circle
and wetted it down
with lake water
from the electric pump
the auger-holes on the beach;
a white goose is the dance
of me, the vatting ice,
the green surface eyes
in the dance, for she seeks
her gone children there,
in this dance;·
goose-thin, the nostrils
like stalks, her sons
shimmering in the lake ice,
goose and crescent
perfect, two figurines.

In this decade I expect
the environment to pull
each into place
as weedbanks giving cover
to my goose.
I stroke her open-ended
neck and watch the air.
To watch my goose in dance,
to watch her fly
and with the breakup ice

in spring, to fish
our children back,
to make them sing before her eyes:
then watch my goose, my dance,
her arching neck a crescent
open-ended.

The Ice-Fishing House

Checking the traps
on the way out
along the iced beaches
the birches sift,
connecting a groundwork
overcome without woman,
this particular snow.

At the first point
the bunny boots soak
up the foot of water
under snow—
we slip in the single
tracks on thick ice
zigzagging northeast
to the house marked "Schultz."

The three trap doors
prism as we auger down,
sinker, minnow, 28 feet;
the kerosene stove heats
the first croppy bed
and we eat.

This greenhouse is set
on stilts, drawn by snowmobiles
over Thanksgiving;
6 × 8 × 6
compass, sextant, wheel
blue light.

Thirty-five crappies in a pail
go with us as we leave this hut;
jackrabbit tracks

cross to the point.
Bunny boot snowshoes or full
fishpail, these traps remain unfilled.

The hollow sounds in this wind,
Kandiyohi, Indian place-names
I've heard in my grandmother's voice
calling the Chippewa in
calling the Chippewa in

Photographs: A Vision of Massacre

We thought the grass
would grow up quickly
to hide the bodies.
A brother sloped across
his brother, the patched
clay road slipping
into our rainy season
of red, our favorite color.

When the pictures came
we spoke of our love
for guns, oiled and glistening
in the rich blood of machines:
bodies, boys and girls, clutching
their private parts, oiled,
now slightly pink,
and never to be used.

"Bird Lives": Charles Parker

Last on legs, last on sax,
last in Indian wars, last on *smack,*
Bird is specious, *Bird* is alive,
horn, unplayable, before, after,
right now: it's heroin time:
smack, in the melody a trip;
smack, in the Mississippi;
smack, in the drug merchant trap;
smack, in St. Louis, Missouri.

We knew you were through—
trying to get out of town,
unpaid bills, connections
unmet, unwanted, unasked,
Bird's in the last arc
of his own light: *blow Bird!*
And you did—
screaming, screaming, baby,
for life, after it, around it,
screaming for life, *blow Bird!*

What is the meaning of music?
What is the meaning of war?
What is the meaning of oppression?
Blow Bird! Ripped up and down
into the interior of life, the pain,
Bird, the embraceable you,
how many brothers gone,
smacked out: blues and racism,
the hardest, longest penis
in the Mississippi urinal:
Blow Bird!

Taught more musicians, then forgot,
space loose, fouling the melodies,

the marching songs, the fine white
geese from the plantations,
syrup in this pork barrel,
Kansas City, the even teeth
of the mafia, the big band:
Blow Bird! Inside out Charlie's
guts, *Blow Bird!* get yourself killed.

In the first wave, the musicians,
out there, alone, in the first wave;
everywhere you went, Massey Hall,
Sweden, New Rochelle, *Birdland*,
nameless bird, Blue Note, Carnegie,
tuxedo junction, out of nowhere,
confirmation, confirmation, confirmation:
Bird Lives! Bird Lives! and you do:
Dead—

Christian's Box Seat: So What!

> A boy and his body
> in a box;
> though his father's
> arm is an ax;
> father and son,
> mother in the morgue,
> and the country
> wholly responsible.
>
> Buried in the desert
> are the true artifacts,
> the slow Nile,
> Osirus on congas,
> a bitch named Isis
> off into revenge.
>
> Alcibiades,
> you're breaking discipline
> baby, it's hard
> to keep on pushing
> when you can't read
> the signs or follow instructions.
> Got a head like a sphinx-nigger—
>
> You'll get a test
> which you'll fail,
> Christian;
> even though you spell
> backwards, and in rage,
> pee down on your
> signifying playmates,
> you ain't gonna make it
> in school,
> less you learn
> to clean up.

And in this man's
gallery, the loss of much
woman, and the images
coming on:
catch it,
on canvas, and on
the sink
'fore the water
runs dry.

Ancestors in African masks
beckon you to this fountain
where your father drinks,
and on the funeral pyre
your mother in this smoke
and a man running.

High Modes: Vision as Ritual: Confirmation

Black Man Go Back To The Old Country
Black Man Go Back To The Old Country
Black Man Go Back To The Old Country
Black Man Go Back To The Old Country

And you went back home for the images,
the brushwork packing the mud
into the human form; and the ritual:
Black Man Go Back To The Old Country.

We danced, the chocolate trees and samba
leaves wetting the paintbrush, and babies
came in whispering of one, oneness,
otherness, forming each man in his music,
one to one: and we touched, *contact-high,*
high modes, *contact-high,* and the images,
contact-high, man to man, came back.
Black Man Go Back To The Old Country.

The grooves turned in a human face,
Lady Day, blue and green, modally,
and we touched, *contact-high,* high modes:
Black Man Go Back To The Old Country.

Bird was a mode from the old country;
Bud Powell bowed in modality, blow Bud;
Louis Armstrong touched the old country,
and brought it back, around corners;
Miles is a mode; Coltrane is, power,
Black Man Go Back To The Old Country
Black Man Go Back To The Old Country
Black Man Go Back To The Old Country

And we go back to the well: Africa,
the first mode, and man, modally,
touched the land of the continent,

177

modality: we are one; a man is another
man's face, modality, in continuum,
from man, to man, *contact-high,* to man,
contact-high, to man, high modes, oneness,
contact-high, man to man, *contact-high:*

Black Man Go Back To The Old Country
Black Man Go Back To The Old Country
Black Man Go Back To The Old Country
Black Man Go Back To The Old Country

Part VII

from *Dear John, Dear Coltrane*

Brother John

Black man:
I'm a black man;
I'm black; I am—
A black man; black—
I'm a black man;
I'm a black man;
I'm a man; black—
I am—

Bird, buttermilk bird—
smack, booze and bitches
I am Bird
baddest nightdreamer
on sax in the ornithology-world
I can fly—higher, high, higher—
I'm a black man;
I am; I'm a black man—

Miles, blue haze,
Miles high, another bird,
more Miles, mute,
Mute Miles, clean,
bug-eyed, unspeakable,
Miles, sweet Mute,
sweat Miles, black Miles;
I'm a black man;
I'm black; I am;
I'm a black man—

Trane, Coltrane; John Coltrane;
it's tranetime; chase the Trane;
it's a slow dance;
it's the Trane
in Alabama; acknowledgment,

a love supreme,
it's black Trane; black;
I'm a black man; I'm black;
I am; I'm a black man—

Brother John, Brother John
plays no instrument;
he's a black man; black;
he's a black man; he is
Brother John; Brother John—

I'm a black man; I am;
black; I am; I'm a black
man; I am; I am;
I'm a black man;
I'm a black man;
I am; I'm a black man;
I am:

For Bud

Could it be, Bud
that in slow galvanized
fingers beauty seeped
into *bop* like Bird
weed and Diz clowned—
Sugar waltzing
back into dynamite,
sweetest left hook you
ever dug, baby;
could it violate violence
Bud, like Leadbelly's
chaingang chuckle,
the candied yam
twelve string clutch
of all blues:
there's no rain
anywhere, soft
enough for you.

Elvin's Blues

Sniffed, dilating my nostrils,
the cocaine creeps up my
leg, smacks into my groin;
naked with a bone for luck,
I linger in stickiness,
tickled in the joints;
I will always be high—

Tired of fresh air,
the stone ground bread,
the humid chant of music
which has led me here,
I reed my song:

"They called me the black
narcissus as I devoured
'the white hopes'
crippled in their inarticulate
madness,
Crippled myself,
Drums, each like porcelain
chamber pots, upside down,
I hear a faggot insult my
white wife with a sexless grin,
maggots under his eyelids,
a candle of my fistprint
breaks the membrane of his nose.
Now he stutters."

Last Thursday, I lay with you
tincturing your womb
with aimless strokes I could not feel.

Swollen and hard the weekend,
penitent, inane
I sank into your folds,
or salved your pastel tits,
but could not come.

Sexless as a pimp
dying in performance
like a flare gone down,
the tooth of your pier
hones near the wharf.
The ocean is breathing,
its cautious insomnia—
driven here and there—
with only itself to love.

Village Blues

The birds flit
in the blue palms,
the cane workers wait,
the man hangs
twenty feet above;
he must come down;
they wait for the priest.
The flies ride on the carcass,
which sways like cork in a circle.
The easter light pulls him west.
The priest comes, a man
sunken with rum,
his face sandpapered
into a rouge of split
and broken capillaries.
His duty is the cutting
down of this fruit
of this quiet village
and he staggers slowly, coming.

The Black Angel

Childhood games,
played without innocence,
and in place of the angel,
take me to a grove of pepper trees;
they lighten my head.
Trees emit their odors,
a natural oxygen tent;
have you noticed the air is heavy
in trees that shed their leaves
without hesitance,
and flow with sap,
and are closest
to the angel's skin;
the eyes, each singly
wide, smarting, unreadable
as the sap, and which
recount the games,
verses, puzzles of other men:
I am reading poems
to this black angel.
Kindled in the shrill
eloquence of other men,
the angel forces open my hands
and in the palms
leaves her footprints.

Clark's Way West: Another Version

The venereal moon
draws six women
to the Missouri River
where they empty their
beaver pelt children
in great Montana falls
near Indian prairie slope.
From the rattler's rattle
their labor was eased
and the children came
from their collective blindness
to the Shawnee burial ground:
each child is blind.
The earth is not invalid here,
the grizzly slaps at salmon,
and stops, and retreats;
and the children bob
down the falls to the basin below.

Effendi

The piano hums
again the clear
story of our coming,
enchained, severed,
our tongues gone,
herds the quiet
musings of ten million
years blackening the earth
with blood and our moon women,
children we loved,
the jungle swept up
in our rhapsodic song
giving back
banana leaves and
the incessant beating
of our tom-tom hearts.
We have sung a long time here
with the cross and the cotton field.
Those white faces turned
away from their mythical
beginnings are no art
but that of violence—
the kiss of death.
Somewhere on the inside
of those faces
are the real muscles
of the world;
the ones strengthened
in experience and pain,
the ones wished for in one's lover
or in the mirror
near the eyes
that record this lost, dogged data
and is pure, new, even lovely
and is you.

Malcolm's Blues

So now we have come
to silence
like an ant-race
in a hidden pimple
while in white America
they squeal with
pleasure and assurance
that you've got your kite
caught in a poplar tree:
it doesn't count.

In Chicago
they commemorate
the slums to your
platform,
and the handkerchief
women weep, and
the guns come out
for the thousandth time.
With the revenge
we watch our admissions
of guilt
sink with the shaft of the wasp,
to kiss the white queen—
ass, nose and elbow.

Remember Mexico

Villages of high quality
merchandise—hand-tooled leather,
blown glass like diamonds,
cloth finer than linen,
delicious food without dysentery,
mountain water from palapa groves
cured by glistening rocks,
burro-drawn carts for the day,
fishing boats destined for clear
water and giant marlin;
the peasants clean
tanned and bilingual;
lemon, papaya,
horseback or raft,
turtle in the picnic
baskets, white lunch
on hacienda siesta—
pure and unblemished
in the public notices.

I remember the birds
of the desert
ripping a horse
not yet fallen;
hookworm, beetles,
the soup of the desert;
cows and donkeys
eat around the cracked
and broken American
automobiles; in this covey
of linkage, spoken here,
I think of Montezuma's
unspeakable rites
in honed rock graves—

bloodmeal and black tunnels;
Indians who speak no Spanish
and worship the sea,
fruit unpicked in suspect
sweetness for corn,
diesel smoke forcing
Indian, and Indian
and Indian, and Indian
farther up the mountainside.

Zocalo

We stand pinned
to the electric mural
of Mexican history
and listen to a paid guide
explain fresco technique
and the vision of Diego Rivera:
Cortes, crippled with disease,
his Indian woman and son,
sailor raping an Indian
in frocks of priesthood.

In the center the Mexican
eagle peels the serpent
and cools his thirst on desert cactus;
Hidalgo forced into Independence,
that bald creole iconoclast
lost east of Guadalajara;
near him, Montezuma
passively meets Cortes,
salutes the Gods,
dies, the mistake of his people;
corn mixes with chickens and goats,
housepets, muskets and cactus wine.

To your left Rockefeller,
Morgan, the atomic bomb,
Wall Street, the pipeline to the Vatican;
below, the Mexican people pay
for the chosen friar
and the dignity of retreat
to the hills above the central valley.

Then comes Juarez—our guide's
voice rings with full-blooded pride

at the full-blooded Indian
busting the military;
he disbands the church,
opens his arms, and gives
the land to the people.
Our guide is speaking in Spanish:
"You see, my friends, we want the land
that Santa Anna gave you for ten
million pesos; we want Texas, Arizona
and the rest of the west;
take the painting, absorb it—
then give us back our land."

Black Spring

We gave it life, mahogany hands,
loose in song;
we gave it to children
in paraffin—
our biology.
It grew lovely and indecent
into a female orchid,
and, of course, produced
children of its own.
We took it back again.

Blues Alabama

She's blacker
than the night which holds
us in our communion
against the white picket fences.
There's clash in her eyes,
and she smiles whitely
to the tambourines.
There's a folk song audience
of rebels who lover
her mother into children,
and then the children,
and they're all in the roads
searching for the art
which makes singing
a blessing of hatred.

American History

Those four black girls blown up
in that Alabama church
remind me of five hundred
middle passage blacks,
in a net, under water
in Charleston harbor
so *redcoats* wouldn't find them.
Can't find what you can't see
can you?

We Assume: On the Death of Our Son,
Reuben Masai Harper

We assume
that in 28 hours,
lived in a collapsible isolette,
you learned to accept pure oxygen
as the natural sky;
the scant shallow breaths
that filled those hours
cannot, did not make you fly—
but dreams were there
like crooked palmprints on
the twin-thick windows of the nursery—
in the glands of your mother.

We assume
the sterile hands
drank chemicals in and out
from lungs opaque with mucus,
pumped your stomach,
eeked the bicarbonate in
crooked, green-winged veins,
out in a plastic mask;

A woman who'd lost her first son
consoled us with an angel gone ahead
to pray for our family—
gone into that sky
seeking oxygen,
gone into autopsy,
a fine brown powdered sugar,
a disposable cremation:

We assume
you did not know we loved you.

Reuben, Reuben

I reach from pain
to music great enough
to bring me back,
swollenhead, madness,
lovefruit, a pickle of hate
so sour my mouth twicked
up and would not sing;
there's nothing in the beat
to hold it in
melody and turn human skin;
a brown berry gone
to rot just two days on the branch;
we've lost a son,
the music, *jazz*, comes in.

Deathwatch

Twitching in the cactus
hospital gown, a loon
on hairpin wings,
she tells me how
her episiotomy
is perfectly sewn
and doesn't hurt
while she sits in a pile
of blood
which once cleaned
the placenta
my third son should be in.
She tells me how early
he is, and how strong,
like his father,
and long, like a black-
stemmed Easter rose
in a white hand.

Just under five pounds
you lie there, a collapsed
balloon doll, burst in your
fifteenth hour, with the face
of your black father,
his fingers, his toes,
and eight voodoo
adrenalin holes in
your pinwheeled hair-lined
chest; you witness
your parents sign the autopsy
and disposal papers
shrunken to duplicate
in black ink

on white paper
like the country
you were born in,
unreal, asleep,
silent, almost alive.

This is a dedication
to our memory
of three sons—
two dead, one alive—
a reminder of a letter
to Du Bois
from a student
at Clark—on behalf
of his whole history class.
The class is confronted
with a question,
and no one—
not even the professor—
is sure of the answer:
"Will you please tell us
whether or not it is true
that negroes
are not able to cry?"

America needs a killing.
America needs a killing.
Survivors will be human.

New Season

My woman has picked
all the leaves,
rolled her hands into locks,
gone into the woods
where I have taught her
the language of these wood leaves,
and the red sand plum trees.
It is a digest
of my taking these leaves with hunger;
it is love she understands.
From my own wooden smell
she has shed her raisin skin
and come back
sweetened into brilliant music:
Her song is our new season.

Dear John, Dear Coltrane

a love supreme, a love supreme
a love supreme, a love supreme

Sex fingers toes
in the marketplace
near your father's church
in Hamlet, North Carolina—
witness to this love
in this calm fallow
of these minds,
there is no substitute for pain:
genitals gone or going,
seed burned out,
you tuck the roots in the earth,
turn back, and move
by river through the swamps,
singing: *a love supreme, a love supreme;*
what does it all mean?
Loss, so great each black
woman expects your failure
in mute change, the seed gone.
You plod up into the electric city—
your song now crystal and
the blues. You pick up the horn
with some will and blow
into the freezing night:
a love supreme, a love supreme—

Dawn comes and you cook
up the thick sin 'tween
impotence and death, fuel
the tenor sax cannibal
heart, genitals and sweat
that makes you clean—
a love supreme, a love supreme—

Why you so black?
cause I am
why you so funky?
cause I am
why you so black?
cause I am
why you so sweet?
cause I am
why you so black?
cause I am
a love supreme, a love supreme:

So sick
you couldn't play *Naima,*
so flat we ached
for song you'd concealed
with your own blood,
your diseased liver gave
out its purity,
the inflated heart
pumps out, the tenor kiss,
tenor love:
a love supreme, a love supreme—
a love supreme, a love supreme—

Molasses and the Three Witches

Inside out, the police announce
there's a riot—on CBS—
it's a barnfire.
Firemen and police
Ball-eye into the squares:
this is the first barnfire
in history.
Roll 'em:
Lady says she saw
the first keg of molasses
in a gunny sack
on a huge black's back;
a black rose bush
on his big-eared helper;
flour and grits
in a pelt as soft as snow—
all gone up in the smoke
of the last spiritual
of Bre'rs Bear,
Rabbit, Fox—
the black trinity:
I will not go quietly—
I will not go quietly—
I will not go quietly—

A Mother Speaks: The Algiers Motel Incident, Detroit

It's too dark to see black
in the windows of Woodward
or Virginia Park.
The undertaker
pushed his body back
into place
with plastic and gum
but it wouldn't
hold water.
When I looked
for marks
or lineament
or fine stitching
I was led away
without seeing
this plastic
face they'd built
that was not my son's.
They tied the eye
torn out
by shotgun
into place
and his shattered
arm cut away
with his buttocks
that remained.
My son's gone
by white hands
though he said
to his last word—
"Oh I'm so sorry,
officer, I broke your gun."

Mr. P. C.

Paul Laurence Dunbar Chambers—
what a long history
of perfection, bass man,
those swollen solos
on Miles's Standard
teachings—"Blues"
dum, dum, dum, dum, dum.

If Mingus is monster
star, you are his
private brother, so soft
baby, so beauteous
in your shuffling,
how many soundful
dysplexia did you do it
over and over and over
do it to everybody's gutstrings
listening as flat out,
Jim, as harpheart and bone—
What a long history
Paul Laurence Dunbar Chambers,
and your namesakes,
in the chambers.

Dead-Day: Malcolm, Feb. 21

The pit-vipers are asleep
having wreathed through
each bullet-hole memory
cued by the new religion:
we are now a black establishment
in our love for you.

It is astonishing
how four years gashed
wider chasms in our story
in our mayflower
and your famous postcard
to PLAYBOY—
Xmas card to follow:
"Happiness by any means necessary."

We've placed some Malcolmesque
soul brothers near the soul kits;
who walks the schizophrenic line?
what is terror but a black orchid,
a white lightnin' bouquet:
St. Malcolm at the Oracle:
A-um-ni-pad-me-hum:
Another brother gone.

Barricades

Barricades hammered into place,
the beams stake out
in broad daylight
to avert nothing
they've taken; the old second
floor where they write the checks,
synchronize the grades,
or type in correct places
a stream data prognosis
is taken in the night;
the magpies are around, around
the corporate desk.

The blacks are studying
the records kept,
memorizing the numbers,
tallying the secret exits,
remembering the names,
the window pipes, outside,
for the way down.

They've gotten up there
with Frederick Douglass
in a six-hour duel
with the overseers,
the first confrontation
to his own man;
Du Bois in Atlanta
looking at the fingers
toes of meat market Sam;
and Malcolm in his first
act crumbling his prison
and the bullet proof glass.

Someone is having a familiar
vision of the black-white syndrome
in the academic halls;
in the cigar smoke
one hears the full-bull
rhesis rhetoric
and the black Christmas
in the halls of ivy:
the barricades come down—

Ode to Tenochtitlan

Socks and gloves
the medal of honor
ablaze in twin fists
of two men
blackened in the imperial fires;
they stand before Coltrane
in their beauty,
the new emblem—
ANOTHER BROTHER GONE—
a style so resilient
and chromatic the pure
reeds of their bodies
bulge through metric
distances in their
special rhythms.
The impossible bowels
of round forms
digest the air
of the television
cameras in
a new vision
now on Olympus;
moon-children,
Gemini, the black stopwatch.

We have heard
the cries
bend the index,
the word-form
plumed black,
the traditional images.
Who can understand
having thought life
was somehow,

transmuted and cleansed
transistored
into a machine.

In the heats,
in the instant replays,
amidst the circuits
of brain waves
come back into
rhythm with a fisted
victory in another
game, a new
current, a new
exchange, a new
vision:
as a twin black spirit,
brother's come on home.

Biafra Blues

Another brother gone
another brother gone
another brother gone
another brother gone
another brother gone
another brother gone

Gray hair and puffed bellies
the stomach moves out
to its specialty—
floating children first,
without smiles
The Soviet Union
lays it out
on the consumers
starving
in the oil slick
whites of their eyes;
the Red Cross
bandages
the refugee
camps in a white
blockade:

another brother gone
another brother gone
another brother gone
another brother gone
another brother gone
another brother gone

Egyptian pilots
cash the American checks—
Lagos, old England,
Washington
are animal kingdoms
in the guts of war:
there is no war
that's not famine
members of the UN

Biafra is an eastern
community in revolt
across territorial lines
worked out with a European
compass: fathom the sectioning
off Biafra—

There is no famine
there is no genocide
only a community
in revolt, only
the refinement of oil
slicks, only a black
smell, sunken, aglow:

another brother gone
another brother gone
another brother gone
another brother gone
another brother gone
another brother gone

Poetry from Illinois

History Is Your Own Heartbeat
Michael S. Harper (1971)

The Foreclosure
Richard Emil Braun (1972)

The Scrawny Sonnets and Other Narratives
Robert Bagg (1973)

The Creation Frame
Phyllis Thompson (1973)

To All Appearances: Poems New and Selected
Josephine Miles (1974)

Nightmare Begins Responsibility
Michael S. Harper (1975)

The Black Hawk Songs
Michael Borich (1975)

The Wichita Poems
Michael Van Walleghen (1975)

Cumberland Station
Dave Smith (1977)

Tracking
Virginia R. Terris (1977)

Poems of the Two Worlds
Frederick Morgan (1977)

Images of Kin: New and Selected Poems
Michael S. Harper (1977)